MEN'S GUIDE TO ROMANCE, INTIMACY AND SEX

Jeffrey Martin

Dedication

To the ones who got away, and the ones who didn't; to opportunities lost and gained; the ones who were so right, and the ones who proved to be so wrong, to the ones I had everything in common with, and those who proved to me I had nothing in common with; to those I wanted to be with and to those who wanted to be with me; to the beauties who I couldn't believe would look at me twice, but who did; to all the ugly women whose outer beauty took my breath away and still does, and to all the truly beautiful women I i didn't look at twice at first; to all women of depth and substance, and to all women of shallowness and superficiality; to everything each one of you taught me about life and love and romance and intimacy; To those who are offended by what I say, or object to my saying it, you all know one thing: everything I say is true. You know this because I learned it all from you.

JEFFREY MARTIN

Contents

INTRODUCTION

It would be nice to think romance has something romantic about it, but it doesn't.

Romance follows strict Principles.

The Principles of Romance are the way they are, not the way I would like them to be. When you learn what they are, they may not be the way you would like them to be. But no matter how much we may wish they were otherwise, they will still be the same.

The Principles of Romance govern the relationship between every man and every woman. There are no exceptions, although, until you completely understand, it may appear that there are.

I know what you don't, not because I'm smarter than you, or more capable than you, but because I went through it all, and learned the Principles of Romance from experience.

I had to.

I had no one to teach me.

You don't have to suffer lost opportunities, rejection, disappointment, disillusion, misunderstandings, or confusion, the way I did.

You have me.

To be successful in romance you need to learn, and utilize The Principles of Romance that all men who are successful with women know and use.

I will teach you these Principles, how to prepare yourself for the challenges they present, how to develop the skills you need, and how to apply them.

You will succeed. That's guaranteed. Because, and here's a secret men who are successful with women all know: Women are more eager for romance than men are.

The reason is quite simple. Throughout human existence women have had an instinctual drive to become pregnant, have children, and to care for them from birth to maturity. So they need a man to protect and provide for them. You don't. Even if a woman doesn't intend children she can't just turn off millennia of inbred need. Most women are smaller, weaker, and, as of this writing, have, on average, less earnings than most men. For that reason a male protector and provider is, a great asset to a safe, secure, prosperous, life for a woman. Not for you. Bottom line: typically, a woman wants a relationship more than a man. But, it must be with a man who's right for her.

Every woman has an imaginary man of her dreams. And, without exception, every man is 'the man of her dreams' to the right woman.

Most women are impaired by a lethal passivity, that is both innate to the female, and reinforced by family, society, and culture. Most women won't take any initiative at all, no matter how lonely they are, no matter how attractive and desirable they think you are, and no matter how much they want to be with you.

In addition to this many women are defensive when they're approached by a man because they're afraid he has bad intentions, and, she thinks, if she allows it, he will take advantage of her, and hurt her. And, unfortunately, there are men who will do just that if they're given the opportunity.

So you must find your woman, make her acquaintance, and show her that you are the man she has been dreaming of.

When you do, she'll want you to win her over.

But you have to take the initiative.

And you must do it in the right way.

To do this you must master The Principles of Romance.

If you do, you will have all the romance, intimacy, and sex you can handle.

You can have a deep, fulfilling, loving, exciting, adventurous relationship. And the woman who is with you, will have the same relationship with you, because when you succeed for yourself you succeed for her also.

Or, you can have many relationships, for as long or short and as deep or superficial as you, and the women in your life, want.

Just one more proviso:

Read the entire book through before you try to interpret anything in it, before you draw any conclusions, before you adapt what I tell you to yourself, before you begin to prepare yourself, before you start to practice, before you start to hone your skills, and before you begin to get experience. The entire book is one integrated body of knowledge, and no one part makes any sense without knowing the whole.

CHAPTER 1

Regardless of what you look like, what kind of physical shape, your athletic ability, your intelligence, your education, your occupation, how much money you have, where you live, how you live, what you like to spend your time doing, what your prospects are, there are women who will find you attractive and desirable, and want to be with you.

You can identify who they are, approach them, establish rapport, and win them, by following The Principles of Romance I am going to lay out for you.

It's actually quite simple if you know what you're doing. There's no trial and error. It's a science, governed by The Principles of Romance.

First Sight

A man knows if a woman will find him attractive and desirable on first sight.

No magic, no chance, no luck.

Whether a woman finds a man who is approaching her attractive or not isn't up to her, it's up to him.

Criteria a woman has no control over determine the type of man she finds attractive and wants for a relationship.

As far as she's concerned a man who's right for her simply materialize out of her dreams and into her reality. That is why women surrender so eagerly to a man who's right for her. But this eager surrender doesn't just happen. You make it happen.

A woman's desire is an irresistible subconscious drive that is felt, not thought. If she tried to verbalize why she finds a certain man attractive and desirable she would say "There's something about him". "Something" is a good enough explanation for her, but not for you.

That "something", that makes you instantly and immediately attractive and desirable to a woman you approach is that you are taller, heavier, and older.

So, obviously a woman who is available to you, who will find you attractive and desirable when you first approach her, is shorter, lighter, and younger than you.

Read on:

Physically you must be a match if you expect a woman you're interested in to be interested in you.

Remember, women respond to what they can perceive, which is, what you look like, not what they can't perceive, which are your qualities, which are important, but come later.

Height

A man must be at least as tall as the woman, but preferably 1 inch to 6 inches taller, but no more, ideally 2-4" taller. Other qualities, such as being a celebrity, or having a lot of money, can offset height, but it's a detriment to be more than 6 inches taller, or any amount shorter than a woman you are interested in, and the shorter you are, or the more over six inches taller, the more you have to overcome in other ways. As an example, to be attractive height wise,, to a woman who is 5'4", you should be between 5'5" and 5'10"' but ideally 5'7". Even if you win her over because of other qualities she will always find men who better fit her height criteria more attractive than you, and this bodes ill for a successful relationship.

Weight

A man must be between twenty and thirty three percent heavier for a woman to find him attractive and desirable. If a woman weighs 120 lb. the man must weigh between 144 lb. and 160 lb. As with height, you can overcome this with other qualities but she will always find men more suitable to her in weight more attractive than you, and this is a problem you don't want.

Age

The man should be at least the same age, ideally 2 years older, but maximally 3 years older. As the man is over 3 years older the chances of a successful relationship diminishes. Relationships in which the woman is more than 12 months older than the man are possible, but rare. So if your objective is success, direct your attention at women your own age, or, up to, but not much more than 3 years younger, but ideally two years younger. A woman in that age relationship to you will find you most attractive. If you do succeed despite an age discrepancy outside that range, the woman, you are in a relationship with, will find men who fit her age range more attractive than you, and you don't want that.

Height, weight, and age, limits the women who are available to you to those who are shorter, lighter, and younger within the range I described.

If you think limiting yourself to women who physically match you in this way, is too limiting, the reality is the only thing you're limiting for yourself is disinterest, rejection, and failure, but you're gaining limitless opportunity.

In every height, weight, and age category there are absolutely stunning beauties, women who couldn't be finer in their outer and inner qualities if you designed them yourself.

Think of women who are not only beautiful but also kind, and gentle, sweet, thoughtful, considerate,and positive in outlook, on your wave length, (assuming these things are what you desire), who will really like you and like being with you, and who you will really like and like being with.

This includes not thousands of women, but millions, far more than you could approach in your lifetime, even if all you did was approach women who will find you attractive and desirable because of your height, weight, and age.

So now you know who you're going to approach.

Now we're going to discuss what you have to do to prepare yourself for a successful approach.

When you approach a woman has to judge you by what she sees. So, you could say women are superficial, but they have no choice. Women can't see inside you.

When a woman sees you approach she's going to have an instantaneous response. If you're appropriately taller, heavier, and older she'll find you attractive and she'll be interested.

Unfortunately, or fortunately, finding a woman who matches you physically isn't the end.

It's the beginning.

CHAPTER 2

This is everything you need to know to give yourself every advantage in making your initial approach to a woman who interests you:

If you are overweight, in poor shape, sedentary, weak, poorly dressed and groomed, with poor posture, low self esteem, poorly motivated, lacking ambition, poorly educated, with little in the way of attainments, few prospects, and little self confidence, you can find countless women who will find you attractive and desirable because they meet the same description, but are shorter, lighter, and younger, and they want to be with a man taller, heavier, and older than they are, and that's you. Women who meet this description will usually be very excited to meet you, and very much want a relationship with you. And that's fine if you are fine with women who meet these criteria.

But it's within you to become a man that truly stunning women will be eager to be with. There's no magic to it, and it's not a secret. All men who are successful with women know what I'm about to tell you.

Women all want the same things in a man.

So I'll tell you what, in addition to the initial criteria of height, weight, and age, are the qualities all women desire.

And once you know what they are, I'll tell you how to be the most attractive and desirable you can make yourself.

So read on:

Women like men who are fit, appropriately dressed and groomed, approach with a sincere relaxed facial expression, who make eye contact, have a nice smile, are decisive, assertive, confident, and have reassuring body language.

You may have all these down pat. If so, just keep it up. But most of us are on a continuum, not great, not terrible.

So let's discuss these things.

First thing to know:

Advance preparation is the key to success.

Everything you do to make yourself visually appealing to a woman is done in advance.

Fitness

Women find men very attractive who are physically fit, trim, at their ideal weight-neither under nor over weight, strong, flexible, well coordinated, and athletic.

How fit you are is within your control.

If you do a daily exercise routine of an hour to two hours a day you will get, and stay in shape, and if you don't put in the time and effort you won't maximize your appeal to women.

This is actually the easiest way to make yourself very desirable to women.

It doesn't have to cost anything. You certainly don't need a gym membership. You can do a complete work out in your home, in your neighborhood, in a park, and you don't need any fancy equipment.

Physical exercise is half of fitness. The other half is proper diet.

Proper diet is divided into quality and quantity. What you don't eat: high fat, high sugar, high cholesterol, prepared foods; and what you do eat: fresh vegetables, beans, seeds, whole grains, nuts, fish, lean meats, and fruits. As to quantity you eat at meal time, without starving or overdoing it. Initially you'll want to gain, or for most, lose, weight, and fat, and gain muscle, but as you shape up, just balance calories burned and consumed. No fancy system is required. Decide what to do from how you look and feel.

If you've never been in good shape, and you get into good shape, you'll be amazed at the difference not just in how great you look and feel, but in how much respect and admiration you get, how much better you will be treated, and how much more attention and desire you get from women.

Unfortunately, if you're not in good shape now, it will take months of physical exercise before you're going to see a significant difference. But others will see a difference, and you'll see a difference in the way people respond to you, almost immediately. It will be a small difference at first, but it will be a big difference as you shape up.

Women want this most of all things they want in a man. So fitness is the one quality that most benefits you in romance.

Think about how you react to a woman who has a beautiful body. That's how a woman reacts to you when you're in shape. Most women won't show that they're wild about you just because you're in good shape, but they are. Not only do they find you attractive and desirable, and want to be with you, they're doing everything in their power to stop themselves from throwing themselves at you, and some women won't stop themselves (as you'll see if you get yourself in shape).

Attire

You may be a very effective dresser. If you are, just keep it up.

But if you're not you can be.

The ideal is to feel comfortable, feel self assured, feel confident, and most important, look on the outside what you are on the inside by giving expression to your personality.

You can dress completely the way you want, if you want to. The advantage is that you'll attract women who like the way you like to dress, and are more likely to like you and be suitable for you. The disadvantage is you're less likely to find a woman who shares your individualistic taste. Because the vast majority of women find attractive whatever standard male attire they're accustomed to.

Women are very narrow minded, extremely shallow, and completely intolerant in appraising your attire. There is an advantage and a disadvantage to this. If you fit her image you're way ahead. If you don't you're not getting anywhere. This might seem foolish but you're wise to understand this and dress accordingly.

The basic question your attire answers for a woman is: "Is he one of us?" (which is good) "or not one of 'us' ?"(which is not good).

If you're not dressed for the place, the situation, what's going on, the people there, and the woman you're interested in, you will probably strike out for that reason alone.

A woman will like the way you look if you look like what her fantasy image of her dream man looks like. And this tends to be in the attire of men she finds attractive. Which is the way the men around her dress.

But remember, if you're dressed, say, as a grungy surfer boy, you'll attract a grungy surfer girl, but you're likely to repel an elegant, chic, sophisticated woman, who might have been attracted to you if you were dressed differently.

As for conformist dressing, just look at how other men are dressed, and without being an exact copy of anyone, dress just like all the other men in the group you want to conform to.

If you're unsure which way to go, for men's attire, conformity rather than originality will get you the best reaction from the most women. But attire is always in relation to the woman you want to attract. Qualitatively there's no difference between a conservative business suit, biker leathers, jeans and t shirt, etc. How you dress can be used for its effect on others.

There is also a concept of over-dressing and under-dressing. Know your occasion, plan for it, and dress accordingly up, or down.

Dressing nicely can be interpreted as a sign of respect and appreciation for the woman in your company, so be aware of that. But don't overdo it. A casual occasion requires casual clothes, a fancy dinner in an expensive formal restaurant requires stylish attire appropriate to the place. There is such a thing as 'smart' casual. Well fitting, good quality, and colors that complement you. And stylish fashionable wardrobe for evening.

If a woman doesn't like the way you're dressed and because of that doesn't like you, tough luck. Or she does like the way you're dressed so she's attracted to you.

Either way, it's the same narrow minded, superficial, attitude, but one way of dressing gets you a good reception and another way a bad reception. Which you get is up to you.

Remember, women aren't going to stop being shallow, because you don't like that they are. So you can use this to your advantage or ignore it and suffer disadvantage.

Of course, the time, effort, and thought you put into your attire is your secret. Never reveal it. It's only the result that counts anyway. If you put a lot into what you wear to a party and you look out of place in a negative way, chalk it up to experience. Figure out what you did wrong, and correct it. Meanwhile while you're there do the best you can. If you get a good reaction from a woman who interests you approach her immediately. (Normally the first man who approaches a woman who's a proper match for her gets her.)

You don't need a lot of money.

Women looking for men with a lot of money will appraise your outfit. These women are experts at it. If you're rich and you look it, women looking for a rich man will come after you. You can take advantage, or not, your choice. But if you're not rich, even if you invested in expensive clothes and shoes, and you did pull off a rich guy act, anything you started with a woman who wants a rich guy will crash and burn as soon as she finds out the truth, so why bother? If all you want is a quick overnight, there's plenty of women in your price category, so don't waste money on clothes and shoes you can't afford.

Clothes and shoes appropriate to your financial means will attract women appropriate to your situation, and (thankfully) repel others, which is what you want, or should want.

If you earn $200,000 a year, don't wear ragged old clothes, just because you don't care about clothes. In fact, don't wear ragged old clothes if you make $20,000 a year. Women don't want to be in a relationship with a bum, so don't look like one. (Even the grunge look varies from cheap to expensive.)

Dress the way you want, individualist or conformist, but know what you're doing and make an intelligent decision.

For purposes of romance the best strategy is to dress for the type of woman who interests you.

Example: If you're a civilized type whose interests run to opera, symphony, ballet, art, look it. You'll repel surfer girls, outdoor types, athletes, but if that's not you why would you want to attract them? They won't like spending time with you anyway. Attract the type of woman who interests you who you will also interest.

Bottom line: dress for the type of woman who interests you, ideally in a way that truly reflects who you are as a person. If you are authentic to yourself it should be the same way. Feel comfortable and self assured, and your attire will work for you.

Be aware that color, fabric, style, and fit can enhance or detract from the way you look. Some men are good at this, others less so. But if you're not you can experiment, see what works, and improve. A few examples: You could improve your look if you have what might be perceived as: a long neck by wearing a turtleneck style; if you are perceived as having narrow shoulders by wearing a sports jacket; if you have a stomach you haven't completely flattened yet by wearing a shirt worn outside your pants; if your arms aren't built up yet by wearing a long sleeve shirt,

Every bit of time and effort you put into your attire will pay you dividends in the positive reaction you get from women who are right for you.

Grooming

You can groom yourself any way you like, longer or shorter hair, whatever style, mustache, beard, close shave, stubble, fingernails, shorter, longer. Any way you like is the ideal.

The way your hair is cut contributes or detracts from your appearance. Figure out what enhances your appearance within the style you prefer. You'll be surprised at how much more attractive you can look with minor styling alterations. But ideally you look like you want to look.

The only really important thing to you is to feel comfortable. The rest doesn't matter to you.

But ideal to you as an individual is not ideal if your aim is romance.

Like attire, looking like you like to look has the advantage of attracting women who are most likely to be compatible with you. But here's the problem: how you groom yourself matters a lot to women. If women who interest you, demand short hair, long hair, clean shaven or stubble, mustache, beard, (ordinarily because that's what her group demands) you have to conform or face rejection.

So, as with attire, you have a choice to be completely yourself in grooming, and possibly attract the most perfect woman for you, but probably suffer rejection by most women.

As with attire, women are intolerant of grooming.

If you want to be accepted, and approved of, by women who interest you, see what the other men look like. Don't copy any individual but conform to the grooming of the other men.

The men in a given situation dress and groom themselves the way they do because it works for them, and it will work for you too.

If you don't conform to norms of attire and grooming you'll usually be considered odd, not one of them, not one of their group, an outsider, someone to be looked at negatively, to be excluded, disliked, avoided. And you don't want that. Nor does it make any real difference to you if your hair is shorter or longer, neatly cut or ragged, if you're clean shaven or stubbly. It means, or should mean, nothing to you, but because it means a lot to women conformity rather than individualism is better for romance.

You'll see the difference when you approach a woman who interests you. In one glance, she instantly forms a favorable or unfavorable impression. If it's favorable you've got the red carpet welcome. If it's unfavorable you're probably not going to overcome her narrow minded, shallow, intolerance.

When you understand, and know how to appeal to the instantaneous positive first impression, and avoid the instantaneous negative first impression, you have plumed the depth of the superficial.

Scent

Women are, nearly always, much more sensitive in their sense of smell than men. They detect scent that a man wouldn't, and they're sensitive to scent a man might detect but ignore.

What this means to you is simply be aware: a shirt you wore all day yesterday might be fine for you to wear today but may very likely be offensive to a woman you approach, so wear only freshly laundered scent free clothing. Don't wear any hair product, cologne, sun screen, insect repellent, deodorant, or other product that has a scent.

To recap: A woman appraises you based on what she can perceive, not what she can't perceive. Of course you are taller, heavier, and older or you wouldn't be walking up to her. Your attire and grooming communicates who you are to her, a hiker, a rock climber, a motorcycle rider, a runner, a surfer, a student at her high school, a lawyer, a doctor, a construction worker, how much money you have. If you have done everything right you have communicated to her that you are someone she wants to associate with (or not, if you mistakenly approach a woman who's not appropriate for you).

A woman will also consider how her friends and social circle will react to her being in a relationship with you-will you be accepted or rejected? will her circle approve or disapprove of a relationship with you?; will her status rise if she enters into a relationship with you?; are you one of 'us'? This analysis takes her a split second. It's felt, not thought.

She looks at you and instantly has all the answers to everything she wants to know. If you have approached a woman who is appropriate for you in the proper way all her answers are: Yes!

You've now identified a woman who interests you, who is appropriately shorter, lighter and younger, than you. You are dressed and groomed properly for the woman and the occasion.

Now we'll go over your approach.

Facial Expression

The way you look at a woman is critical to the reception you get from her.

This is completely within your control.

Your facial expression starts from the inside. Be relaxed, be confident, be strong and gentle, be firm, be friendly, be assertive, be respectful, be interested in her as a woman and as a person, be interested in making her acquaintance, be yourself, and be open. All these things will show on your face. Put an appropriate smile on your face (not a grin or smirk), make eye contact, but don't stare, be responsive to her response.

Your face must reassure her you are friend not foe, protector not predator, assertive (which women like) not aggressive (which women don't like).

Very few women can resist eye contact and a nice, appropriate smile, from a man who is approaching them (assuming you are appropriately taller, heavier, older, attired and groomed in relation to her).

If you look a woman over you'll get a very cold reception, and you'll never overcome it. Even if you meet a woman who's essentially naked, say in a thong bikini on the beach, you look at her body you'll get the brush off. The woman's thought is: 'if you're interested in me as a person you wouldn't be looking at my body.' It's a game women play. They do everything they can to put themselves on display, but they're offended if you look at what they're showing. Eye contact and a sincere smile on your part is your first introduction, and it's critical. A good rule is: 'Don't look below the chin'. If you limit your look to her face you'll likely get the full view soon enough.

She's not walking around the beach in a thong bikini because she wants to go home alone tonight. She wants a man.

But whether it's you is up to you, not her.

Her response is instinctive and patterned. Your actions are intelligent and practiced. Because of this you're in control. (Don't ever say anything about that, it's unspoken.)

Body Language

Stand straight not rigid, be relaxed, but don't slouch.

Be confident, not arrogant, be strong but gentle, inculcate into your mind that you will get a good response from the woman you're approaching (it's a self fulfilling expectation), and your body language will communicate that.

Be decisive, but not aggressive or pushy. Remember you are trying to reassure her that you are friend not foe, that your intentions are good, not evil, that you are courteous, considerate, thoughtful, strong and gentle, respectful, relaxed, and confident.

Non Verbal Communication

Warning: Women are sensitive to non verbal communication, often acutely sensitive. Facial expression, body position, movements, change in relative position or distance, a man wouldn't notice or, if he did, wouldn't pay attention to, communicate a great deal to a woman. To her, non verbal communication is likely to be interpreted as more transparent and more honest than anything you say.

You can use this to your advantage. Just think positive thoughts: You are approaching a woman to get to know her, and for her to get to know you; your intention is to be an excellent man for her; to make her happy she made your acquaintance; to be a positive element in her life, and that you can accomplish this because of your good qualities (in relation to her). And this will all be communicated to her in your non verbal communication.

There are men who are quite successful thinking one thing and communicating another to women. They're pathological liars, natural frauds, or devious predators, so what they communicate does flow 'honestly' from within. They 'honestly' want to deceive their victim. The victim can't sense dishonesty because to such a man there is no sense of honesty or dishonesty to detect. They 'honestly' say what they think will work in the situation they're in without any thought to what is true and what is not. Men like this can get past a woman's internal lie detector test, because making things up doesn't cause them any stress. For men like this their facial expression, body language, and tone of voice are all masterfully in service of deceit, and they usually succeed in fooling their victims.

Even if you're not naturally deceitful you could try to pull this off. But it's unlikely you will succeed. Most men are rather transparent in their thoughts and intentions.

Example:

A man approaches a woman after a soft ball game. He's attracted to her because she has big breasts and he wants to have sex with her not just today but as soon as possible, one time, and then dump her, because say, she's not attractive enough for him, or she's too heavy for his taste, or she's unintelligent, not stylish, or vulgar, or whatever. She asks him; "Why did you come over to talk to me?" and he answers "Because you play a great game, you're a great competitor, you won the game for your team, and I want to recruit you for a league I'm starting with the idea of having all the best players." All lies but quite persuasive because she is an excellent softball player, she did win the game for her team, she would be a good recruit, and he may, or may not, be starting a new league. Since the man in question is naturally deceitful from within himself, he avoids all the usual clues that she looks for. Once he gets past her defenses, he makes rapport, suggests, say, lunch in his apartment, then makes what happens seem spontaneous.

But for most men, a thought or intention like that, would appear blatantly obvious to most women, they would be deeply offended, and would very likely turn the other women against him, by warning them that he approached her in an offensive disrespectful way, that he attempted a transparent subterfuge to get her to his apartment, that she wants nothing to do with him, and suggests they shouldn't have anything to do with him either. Then, when the new softball season starts he discovers he hasn't been picked for any team, and none of the women want to join his league if he starts one.

So put into your mind positive, constructive, considerate, respectful, supportive, thoughts. Be sincere by making them sincere. Sincerity will come through.

And, in the example, if the woman doesn't interest you, don't be, or try to be, devious and exploitive. Be friendly with her, but focus your attention on someone else.

Note: There are women who are extremely sexually active. As long as you're discretely honest about what you want an invitation to lunch in your apartment is fine. Your invitation will be either accepted or rejected, but no harm is done.

Confidence

Women are very attracted to men who show confidence.

They are repulsed by nervousness, anxiety, fear, low self esteem. To women these are very unmanly characteristics and they find them very unattractive. Women interpret these signs as indicating that the man is weak, unintelligent, incompetent, a failure. You wouldn't want to associate yourself with such a man either. If that's what you're signaling and women reject you, now you know why. And if you've been walking up to women with an empty bluster and getting a good reaction you also know why.

Women think that men who display confidence have been successful in their endeavors in the past, are successful in their endeavors now, and expect, for good reason, to be successful in their endeavors in the future. They believe that confident men are strong, intelligent, capable, and effective. They find this very attractive, in fact irresistible.

What they think is absurd.

An image of self confidence is completely independent of anything for which a man might have reason to have self confidence. Many of the most incompetent failures appear like inflated blowhards to men, but come across as confident successes to women, whereas many brilliant successful men don't project a confident image simply because they're quite modest.

It doesn't matter if you are, or consider yourself, a success or a failure, adequate or inadequate, able to handle situations that come up, or unable. Your capabilities or lack of capabilities has nothing to do with projecting self confidence.

Self confidence is an image you project, entirely independent of any objective criteria.

Projecting confidence is an act. A lot of men are inflated bags of hot air naturally, and project confidence because of their inflated conceit, but many men don't. But it's critical that you do, so you have to, whether you want to or not, whether you feel confident or you don't.

You can learn to project confidence. There are, and can be, no excuses.

But remember this is the opposite of arrogance. She must think highly of you, not think that you think highly of yourself.

Projecting confidence and projecting modesty go together.

Don't ever be boastful. If there's something you want her to know that you think will impress her you have to communicate it subtly and modestly.

You show her what your qualities are, you don't tell her what they are.

She must think that you are capable, in control, able to handle whatever comes up, you can't tell her you are.

How do you project confidence if you don't feel confident?

Most important, recognize that you're putting on an act, like an actor. And like a good actor, the performance comes from within. You tell yourself: "I can do this"/"I can handle this"/"I'll do fine"/"She should like me"/"She'll be happy I approached her".

And it usually works out that way because confidence is a self fulfilling prophecy.

If you walk up to a woman who's right for you, and show confidence that she'll respond favorably to you, most often, (but not always,) she'll respond favorably. But if you don't step up to the plate because you're afraid you'll strike out, you can't play ball.

When you project confidence you're non-verbal message is: "I am a very attractive and desirable man, I am very nice to talk to and to be with. I am interested in you because you appear to have many good qualities. I would like to introduce myself to you and I hope you will introduce yourself to me. I would like to get to know you, and I hope you will want to get to know me. I'm a very good person, and I am a very good person to know. I'm sure we'll both be happy if you give me a chance, and if you do you'll be happy you did."

A woman you approach receives and understands this entire non verbal message instantly by looking at you, she likes it, it's what she wants you to communicate to her, and she will respond well to it.

Assertive Not Aggressive

You must be assertive, or you will get nowhere. You must put yourself forward, take reasonable chances, and trust your abilities.

This is the opposite of being aggressive. Never be pushy, forceful, bullying, or threatening. Don't crowd, and never block a woman into a space.

Women are impressed by male assertiveness, they like it, and are attracted to it, but they are fearful of aggressiveness, are repulsed by it, and avoid it.

Almost every woman you will ever encounter thinks that if a man is interested in her he will approach her. If you don't she assumes you're not interested in her. Women are flattered by a man's interest, and, if it's done right, they like it.

When you first walk up to a woman she will instantly see that you are appropriately taller, heavier, and older, in excellent physical shape, well dressed and groomed for the situation, made eye contact with her, have a nice smile. and reassuring posture, are assertive and confident, strong looking and gentle in approach, so she will find you attractive and desirable. She won't think "This man is attractive and desirable", she'll feel it. She'll be flattered by your interest, and she'll be interested in you. She'll want to know who you are, what you're all about, and what you want.

And this gives you your opening.

'Good Looking' Men

A note on being 'good looking'. It doesn't hurt to have looks that women find very good looking.

But this isn't as far out of your control as you might think. A man in good physical shape looks very attractive to a woman. So if you are, or get yourself, in good shape I guarantee you will look attractive to women. Add to this appropriate attire and grooming, add relaxed, friendly, reassuring, assertive, confident approach, eye contact, and smile, and you will have no problem.

Two more aspects of men who are 'good looking':

First, assuming there was something objective about male appearance from the female perspective (which there isn't), you will find that if asked to rank ten men in terms of how 'good looking' they are ten women will rate the same ten men differently (assuming they are all in good shape). Second, you will find women routinely select less 'good looking' men over 'better looking' men for romantic relationships because other qualities outweigh being 'good looking'. Third, you will find that, even if you consider yourself an average looking man (whatever that is), you will find that from time to time, you will encounter a woman who, for unknowable reasons, will find you devastatingly handsome and desirable, and will want to be with you very badly and will show that to you.

Whatever you look like you'll do fine.

CHAPTER 3

You have diligently prepared yourself, identified a woman who is a perfect match for you, made eye contact, pleasant smile, acted decisively, walking right over, projecting friendliness and confidence.

Now what?

You're going to introduce yourself.

So let's discuss what you're going to say, how you're going to prepare for what you're going to say, how you're going to say it, what your immediate objective is, what your goal is, and how you're going to get there.

First Conversation

If you find it easy to speak to women you don't know, and routinely elicit a good response, just keep doing what you're doing.

But most men find it somewhat difficult to speak to women they don't know. Because they find it difficult they don't take advantage of opportunities to speak to women they don't know. It takes practice and it takes experience to improve. So if you're like most men and you're not that good at speaking to women you don't know your first objective is to learn how.

The key to effective conversation is preparing what you will say before the opportunity to say it arises.

Don't memorize the words, it will make you seem phony, insincere, awkward. Formulate ideas, topics, and general words you will use. Be sincere.

There is absolutely nothing insincere about preparing what you will say in conversation in advance. Of course you never mention that you did, because that sounds like you're insincere, and no one likes that.

The basic thrust is that you're approaching to introduce yourself, to establish contact, and to learn something about her, to let her know something about you, beginning with the superficial, and gradually going on from there, to shared interests, activities, experiences, likes, dislikes, etc. You've approached her to get to get acquainted, so your conversation will flow along those lines. But you will never be intrusive or interrogating. She might be excited to talk about recent movies, and no interest in talking about books, or vice versa. So be ready to raise and drop topics smoothly and quickly.

Normally you lead in with innocuous, harmless, unobjectionable topics you have in common, such as how nice the garden behind the church looks, how meaningful the sermon you just heard was, the weather, weather prediction, how beautiful the bride looked, how well the five year olds played soccer. Be positive.

The object of conversation is to talk about what interests the person you're talking to, that also interests you. (If there isn't anything, the person you're trying to talk to isn't right for you.)

The more you know about what does, or might, interest the person you are going to talk to, the better you can prepare.

A good tip is to think up ten topics (or more) so you can bring something up (say a movie you saw last night), drop it and move to something else, if there's no interest.

You must be aware of what's happening around you: popular culture, TV, on line media, celebrities, music, sports, current events, dance, movies, theater, literature, politics, economics, religion. Whatever interests women who interest you. The more current the better. Say, a movie that came out last night is better than bringing up a movie that came out a month ago.

It's mostly common sense. If you go to a hiking club meeting the women there are probably interested in scenic hikes, new equipment, new technology you stumbled on, a good place to shop for high quality equipment at reasonable prices, a great tasting trail food you just discovered; if you go to a ski club meeting women there are probably interested in ski locales, noteworthy new equipment, nice places to ski, a very nice well situated lodge that's reasonable in price, good places to eat in ski areas that are not expensive-perhaps a little off the beaten path, etc. Don't expect a woman at a hiking club meeting to be interested in skiing or a woman at a ski club meeting to be interested in hiking. It should be something new, not well known, useful, of immediate application.

Women are interested in what effects them at the moment, so a place nearby that's extremely scenic, has good hiking terrain, is easy to get to, and not well known, would likely interest a woman interested in hiking. Whereas a trail you found on vacation two years ago, 1,000 miles away, less so, or not at all-unless she's getting interested in you and, possibly, joining you on an adventure like that in the future.

The more immediate and more definite the topic's effect on the woman you're speaking to, the more interest you'll get.

You should have interests that you focus on and develop as much as you can. How interesting and entertaining a subject is depends more on how it's presented than on what it is. A fascinating subject can be turned into a bore. Think: college textbook on any subject. A subject that might seem like a bore, say a chess tournament, can be fascinating. Think: a good Hollywood movie.

Having interesting experiences is the best way of having interesting things to talk about.

If you like hiking, running, skiing, cooking, chess playing, traveling, painting portraits, photographing landscapes, writing poems, whatever, do it, and, as appropriate, in a modest way, discuss it.

Use clues to select what you're going to lead in with. The place, such as a hiking club meeting, the occasion, say a meeting on say, re-routing a trail, or locating a new shelter, are obvious indications of what a woman is interested in. But her appearance, attire, level of fitness, will also help to guide you. And you'll get better at figuring out what might interest a woman you're meeting for the first time as you gain more experience.

As an example, there's nothing wrong with saying: "I've taken up a hobby of photography, would you like to see some pictures I've taken lately?" (Just be sure they're good ones that couldn't possibly be offensive, say flowers, sunsets, landscapes, views from cliff sides, action pictures, from a kayak, etc.)

If you have an interesting occupation bring it out sooner rather than later. Say: "My job is to find locations for photo shoots, commercials and movies. I'm looking for rooftop places now. I had no idea there are so many fabulous rooftop bars, restaurants, clubs," then describe some of them.

It's also good to learn about what interests you from books, journals, magazines, videos, etc. It gives you more to talk about, makes you more interesting, and gives you a wider net to catch a woman's interest.

Even a little bit of time each day in which you study a subject that you find interesting and worthwhile makes you a more interesting and valued man.

What you choose depends entirely on you.

While you should prepare specifically for anticipated situations, like going to a baseball game, or a kayak trip to the Norwalk Islands, or whatever, overall you should choose what interests you, not what you think a hypothetical woman might find interesting because some women are interested in everything you might be interested in, and of course, others are not. But that's part of the value in this: you interest women who share your interests and are good for you, and you lose the interest of women who don't share your interests and are not good for you.

So don't feel badly if you share something interesting to you, say a once in a decade appearance of a comet later that night, when it's predicted to be dark and clear, and she has no interest, brushes you off, and walks away. Consider yourself lucky she didn't indulge you because she's interested in you because you have a lot of money, or you're a movie director, or you have a beach house. You saved yourself a lot of misery. She's not right for you and you're rid of her. So be glad.

Make your scope as wide as you can master but no wider. Say, for example, astronomy, or the constellations, or meteorology, or computer games, or coding, or current books, or movies, or baseball, or whatever.

Just remember, don't be didactic-meaning don't lecture, and don't be boring. Communicate what you know to someone assuming they are intelligent, don't know much about the subject, and don't care to learn much about it. But, if you make what you are saying directly relevant to them, concise, and brief they will likely be interested.

Example, if meteorology is your field of interest, after a destructive tornado is predicted to hit your area, a brief explanation of how the tornado formed, where and when it formed, how it gained its destructive power, its probable route, what someone might do if it does hit, and why and when it will likely come to a stop, could win you rapt attention.

But don't get so rapped up in what you're saying that you miss signals from the woman you're speaking to. If she says: "How do you know so much about tornadoes?" and you're a student of meteorology at say, your state university tell her so. She might be interested in what it's like to be a residential student there (if you are). Try to respond to what she says, follow her interests, and no matter how powerful your interest in tornadoes, they served their purpose, so drop them, and move on to what it's like to live on campus. And try to get her talking. Listen to her carefully, what she says, her tone of voice, her choice of words, watch her facial expression, and her body language, so you can guide yourself on the path of her interests.

If you are not naturally smooth, relaxed, and naturally attuned to speaking to women you don't know, you'll find that it's going to take you time to prepare yourself with things to say, and that, even with adequate preparation, you are somewhat clumsy and perform somewhat awkwardly. But this is part of the learning process. There's no way around it. You'll get better as you practice and gain experience.

Another way to improve at conversation, besides relating your interests to a woman in a way you try to make entertaining, is to research and learn what you think will be interesting to the type of woman you expect to be in contact with. You will get better at this as you get experience. The key is always what is directly relevant to her. If she likes restaurants: a great new restaurant you went to last night; if she likes trail running: a great new trail you just discovered that's not far away; if she's sensitive, a book of truly moving poetry you just read; Just be ready to drop any subject that doesn't elicit interest and try something else.

You needn't have a scintillating opening line.

That's a myth.

If you do have an appropriately amusing comment, or you just say exactly the right thing at the right moment so much the better. But if she's interested, and she will be, anything you say, including "Hello, my name is…………what's yours?" will work just fine.

If the woman you're interested in looks at you, and she's available, and she sees a man who is appropriately taller, heavier, older, attractively dressed and groomed, with a pleasant, relaxed, manly demeanor, assertive (not aggressive), decisive (not pushy), a friendly reassuring facial expression, projecting confidence, making eye contact, with nice posture, she's going to be interested in knowing what you're all about. You're definitely a match for her. She already knows that. You may, (or may not) be the man of her dreams, her special someone. But she's going to want to find out if you are. Because you say "Hello, my name is……." she's not going to lose interest.

Who Is More Important Than What

As long as you're following the Principles (superficial, innocuous, directly relevant, delivered with pleasant facial expression, relaxed body posture, and eye contact) who you choose to speak to is more important than what you say. If you get a good response you've chosen wisely, and if you're getting a poor response you've chosen unwisely.

Always remember, you may be trying to talk to someone who's simply not a good match for you. Shorter, lighter, younger, attire and grooming, are only the beginning. A woman's intelligence, sophistication, education, financial situation, world view, character, personality, and interests, may or may not be a match for you.

If a woman is interested in you she'll be interested in whatever you're saying, and if she isn't, the most scintillating conversation won't interest her in the least, unless of course she sees some immediate benefit to herself in what you're saying. And why would you want to be used by a woman who's not interested in you?

But you'll get better at picking out who to talk to and what to talk about as you get more experience.

Important proviso: always be polite (not shy), respectful (not submissive), considerate, and thoughtful, and never, no matter what the circumstances or situation, ever say anything offensive, aggressive, unkind, or vulgar. If you don't get the response you want just politely break off and move on. But don't be too hasty. Women are sometimes shy, caught off guard, have difficulty talking to men they don't know, feel initially uncomfortable, initially unconnected to you, sometimes have low self esteem, or negative body image, or have had bad experiences in such situations and are fearful and defensive. If she seems interested but shy or fearful just be gentle, encouraging, interested, and supportive. But if you can't break through just move on.

You will get responses that are positive, which is what you will usually get if the woman was selected properly and is available, but you will also get responses that are dismissive, abrupt, uninterested, usually because the woman you approached isn't available, or you made a mistake evaluating her for appropriateness. This can happen because ordinarily you will have a split second to decide whether to approach or not. Remember, usually the first appropriate man who approaches an available woman gets her, so you have to act decisively.

Occasionally you will get an insulting or abusive response to your approach. Fortunately, it's rare but it can happen. First, don't internalize it. That is, don't feel less of yourself. It's her problem not yours. You are what you are, no more no less, and nothing anyone says will ever change that. You are reading this book because you are a striver and that's a good thing. Second, you communicate by your face and body that her comments mean nothing to you, which is what negative comments should mean to you. Then move on. Later, she might find out there's something about you that makes her want to be with you. Say, you're a movie director, you cast models for fashion shows, you manage bands, you're in a band, you're an event planner, you're rich, etc. She'll make it her business to catch up with you, and turn on the charm. Take advantage of the situation if you want, but remember, no matter how beautiful and sexy she might be, she's an ugly, venomous snake, she always will be, she'll poison any relationship she gets into, and any long term relationship will be toxic.

CHAPTER 4

PRACTICE

If you're not smooth and relaxed talking to women you don't know, practice speaking to a woman you don't know whenever you have an appropriate opportunity.

Make eye contact first, show her a nice relaxed appearance, an appropriate little smile, if she returns the look, proceed, if she turns away, stop.

Even a few sentences are fine.

Say you come to an office with no windows, the receptionist tells the person you've come to see that you've arrived for your appointment, and asks you to have a seat. Instead of just quietly sitting down you could say something about the weather. Say, it looked like it was going to rain but the sun came out, or it started to rain just as you entered the building.

At a bus stop waiting for the bus, "According to my App the bus will be here in four minutes"-no reply: don't say another word, positive reply: continue. If she seems encouraging if she sits where you can't join her just go elsewhere; if she sits where you can, ask her if you can sit there. Even if you're not particularly interested in the woman, or if she's not a match for you (but close), it's still a good opportunity to practice speaking to a woman you're meeting for the first time.

To get started stay relevant: i.e. you're reserved seat at a basketball game happens to be next to an appropriate woman, who looks interesting to you, who's at the game with another woman: if she returns your pleasant look you could mention something like "The home team is a ten point underdog but the team's really starting to come together, the've been playing better every game for the last three weeks." (You know this either because you're a fan, or because you looked it up as soon as you knew you would be going to the game. At worst you could discuss what you looked up with the friend who invited you.) If she's not interested in what you say she's not interested in you, so stop.

A note of caution: don't stray too far in any direction, i.e. age, height, weight, etc. If you do it will go poorly for you.

Second note of caution: Always be polite, courteous, respectful, and in the beginning, innocuous, superficial, and positive. Of course, the standards in a dance club are more relaxed than in church, or school, or at work, but the principle is the same.

Third note of caution: In your own neighborhood, church, or place of work, be extremely polite, courteous, and respectful because you'll be constantly seeing the same women, their friends, family, and co-workers, so you don't want any, even possibility, of misunderstanding to arise. In general, don't say anything for or against anyone or anything, be completely positive, and, if you can, get the woman talking, listen, understand, and reply appropriately.

Fourth note of caution: You may encounter women who not only don't want to talk to you, they're hostile to you. Be courteous, polite, and respectful if you have to speak to them, but keep what you say to the minimum, only when necessary, and otherwise leave them be. Never confront them, that only makes it worse.

If you think other men have a natural ability to speak to women they don't know, that you somehow lack, that's, sometimes, but, rarely true. In most cases other men learned through trial and error, and much practice, and you can learn also.

If you prepare things to say, select an appropriate woman and appropriate opportunity, approach with a friendly relaxed demeanor, eye contact, and an appropriate little smile, and speak to her, you may be a little halting, stilted, unnatural, and not terribly engaging in the beginning. It might even cause you some mild embarrassment. But, if you're relaxed, take whatever happens in stride, behave politely and respectfully (never submissively), and analyze what you did correctly-and got a positive response, and what you did incorrectly-and got a negative response, you'll improve.

The difficulty of going from where you are now to where you are capable of being is the Rite of Passage. It's painful, time consuming, emotionally challenging, mentally and physically demanding, uncomfortable, and frustrating, but there's no other way.

You may not believe me now, but after a while you will easily converse with any woman in a relaxed, confident, and engaging manner. Then you'll think back at how hard it was for you, in the beginning, and marvel at how easy it really is. You'll wonder why you found it so difficult to do something so easy.

When you reach this point (and you will), other men, who have difficulty talking to women they don't know, will look at you as a man with a natural ability they lack.

CHAPTER 5

*WOMEN WHO ARE, AND
ARE NOT, AVAILABLE*

You can assume that any woman who isn't currently in a relationship is available.

At times a woman may not be thinking of a relationship. But ordinarily that won't prevent her from responding to you if you are a desirable match for her, and you approach her in an appropriate way.

If you approach a woman who is looking for a relationship, particularly with a man like you, in the right way, you are in.

Detecting whether a woman is available, and available to you, is one of the skills that men who are successful with women all share. It comes naturally to some men. But even if it doesn't come naturally to you, it's a skill that most men can develop. Even if you're one of the few men who simply can't, you can get around it. I'll explain how to develop the skill and, if you can't develop it, how to get around it.

The easiest situation is when you make eye contact and she meets your look, you smile and she smiles back, you walk toward her and she turns toward you with a look of anticipation, that she's glad you're approaching her.

But many women who would like to meet you are shy, fearful, defensive, have low self esteem, or negative body image of themselves, or all those things. So if she looks away or turns away it's not necessarily over. She may be hoping you come over to her but is too afraid or too clumsy to show it.

If she stays where she is, and could, but doesn't do anything to discourage or prevent you from approaching her, go ahead and try, but be ready to push on or back away based on her reaction.

If she seems upset or distressed that you're approaching her don't get any closer, move away from her, and on to someone else.

If she walks away from you, or joins a group with her back to you, move on to someone else.

There is an entire body of knowledge on the subject of body language and how postures and gestures can be interpreted. Such things as crossed arms supposedly indicates a defensive posture, but you'll find it's just as often a comfortable place for a person to put his or her arms. Interpreting body language is more intuitive than scientific.

You can approach a woman in a defensive posture unless she seems hostile to being approached. Be nice, say something innocuous, and if you get an encouraging response continue and if not, move on.

Overall this is a numbers game. As I say, you might find the one and only woman you want, who also wants you, as her one and only man, the first time you approach a woman (after you finish reading this book), or you might not find a woman who you want to have a relationship with and who wants a relationship with you, until you've approached countless women.

And approaching what may turn out to be countless women is how you get around your difficulty in figuring out if a woman is available or not. But as long as you're following The Principles your interactions with women will be positive, you'll meet a lot of attractive interesting women, you'll get better at interacting with women, you'll probably make friends with at least some of them, you'll enhance your reputation as a nice man to be acquainted with, and sooner or later you will meet a woman (or more than one) who finds you attractive and desirable, who wants to be with you, and who is available to you.

Religion

It's a good idea to give a few moments thought to religion.

Probably all religions are true, and it doesn't matter what religion you're a member of.

Do what you feel is right for you, but for simple, stress free, successful, adaptation to life I recommend that you follow the rituals, doctrines, teachings, and attendances of your birth religion. But that is entirely up to you.

As for romance, formal religion isn't important per se, unless you or the woman who interests you finds it so, in which case it is. You meet a Mormon woman, who interests you, but who's dedicated to engagement and marriage to a Mormon. That's her decision, and you respect that. Of course, if you're Mormon you occupy an excellent position with her.

Church services and church events like say, youth groups, volunteer charitable work, social events like barbecues, are an excellent place to meet women, often women with high character and values, and meeting you at a church function usually gives you a major advantage in making you more interesting and desirable to her.

Also, if you share an interest in the church, its doctrines, rituals, faith, values, and attendance, this could be of decisive importance. You may find that a woman will be eager to be with you because you share this aspect of life with her.

In so far as you are concerned you are at liberty to seek out a woman of your own formal religion, even to do so exclusively if you so desire. That's entirely up to you. If you believe that is the correct thing to do, than for you it is correct, and as long as you don't lead anyone else on with false hopes, you can restrict your search for romance to women of your formal religion, and, at least some women do the same thing. They may never tell you why, but you'll never get anywhere with some women because you're not a member of their religion. If that happens, and if you meet enough women it will, just move on.

Subconscious Association

There is a very odd psychological phenomenon you should be aware of, although there isn't anything you can do about it.

Something about you may trigger a subconscious association with someone else in a woman's past, whom she has a positive or negative feeling about.

As an example, you may look, sound, or move like someone who was abusive to her in the past, possibly even as a child. She doesn't think this consciously. She just feels very uneasy in your presence, there's 'something' about you she doesn't like and feels threatened by, and she wants to get away from you. You will never know why, and she won't either. It's the subconscious association, and it can't be overcome.

Fortunately, it works in both directions. She may subconsciously associate your appearance, your tone of voice, your movements with someone who she felt very loving toward, possibly someone from her early childhood. She immediately has a very good feeling about you, she feels safe and secure in your presence, she has an immediate trust in you, she likes you, and hopes to spend time with you. You'll probably never know why, and she won't either. But it's the subconscious association. Only this time it works for you. All you have to do is reinforce her good feelings about you by using the techniques I describe to you.

Human Factors

There is an intangible in relationships.

On paper you might be a perfect match.

Think of Prince Charles and Princess Diana.

But there are aspects of personality, and how personalities respond to each other, that can't be objectified or quantified.

They can be explained, but there really isn't anything you can do about it.

The intangible in personality arises over time.

It is said that it is possible to determine an adult's personality by that person's behavior as an infant. Some infants play quietly and calmly, others are constantly crying, some focus intently, others flit from one thing to the next. Some are very adaptable, others easily disturbed. Some are very warm and cuddly, others cold and distant. Some are very outgoing and trusting, others shy and retiring, fearful of anyone other than parents.

Then come the role of parents, some of whom are neglectful or emotionally cold or uncaring, self absorbed, others who are over protective, or who worship their child as some extraordinary being, and every possible permutation, from demanding, authoritative parents, to abusive, to completely lax, to the ideal parents.

Then comes the role of siblings, home, neighborhood, peers, school, etc.

Minor physical attributes can have major impact on the development of a child into an adult. A slight, almost unnoticeable neurologic abnormality, seen as clumsiness, a learning disability, like dyslexia-a sister with dyslexia, vision or hearing problems, etc.

The role of relative intelligence. A child gets all A's in school with little effort, while another is barely passing despite considerable effort.

Tone of voice. A male with a feminine sounding voice, a female with a male sounding voice, or a speech impediment, or a voice perceived as very attractive.

Relative size in relation to others in the same age category.

Perceived attractiveness. The world is adoring and welcoming to those considered attractive but cold and dismissive to those considered unattractive.

Think of an example: A girl's father was abusive and violent to her and her mother. He was never home except to steal money and keepsakes to sell to buy liquor and gamble. A cheat and a liar, whose appearance in the home was a dreaded event, filled with terror and pain. When a man comes along who drinks alcohol or gambles, even small amounts, or has something of a temper when things don't go his way, or has anger management problems, or whose method of solving a disagreement is to be physically assaultive, it's extremely likely, that no matter how right they seem on paper, they're totally wrong for each other. On the other hand, a man comes along who, on paper, isn't ideal for her, but who is, because he's calm, considerate, caring, a hard worker, who saves his money, who doesn't drink alcohol at all, and doesn't gamble, even so much as a small stakes neighborhood poker game. Of course this same man could be a total reject for a female 'party animal' who lives to drink alcohol, smoke marijuana, sniff cocaine, dance, go to clubs, whose favorite place on Earth is Las Vegas, from which her trip is a success if she's drunk, high, partied, laid, and broke. (And there are plenty of men out there who are perfect for her, and maybe you're one of them.)

Incidentally, what could make a female party animal? Could it be a single mom, who worked herself to exhaustion sixty hours a week to support four kids on her own, came home and washed, cooked, and cleaned for them in her 'free time', never complained once, and died at age fifty of a heart attack?

Of course, these are extreme examples, but, while women are patterned thinkers (think, height, weight, age, attire, grooming, facial expression, eye contact, assertiveness, confidence, establishing rapport with superficial conversation), they are individuals also.

Sterling qualities improve your odds, and defects diminish them, but there is a woman for every man, even one who drinks alcohol to excess, gambles more than he can afford, and has a violent temper.

But this is the human factor which you have no real control over, but which you shouldn't ignore.

If you're not getting anywhere with a woman, if you've done everything right, don't bother questioning yourself. The 'problem' is beyond your control (and hers). Just move on.

A brief note on moving on: never be insulting, abusive, sarcastic or in any way negative. Just "Have a nice day"/ "Nice talking to you"/"I have to get going"/ etc. Whatever is appropriate to the circumstances.

It might help you to think that a woman you approach will tell every other woman about your interaction. So you want it to be positive. The woman you approached may not be interested in you at the moment but ten of her friends might.

CHAPTER 6

Assume you have identified a woman who will find you attractive and desirable, approached her in the proper way, and begun a conversation, which seems to be evoking a positive response from her.

You reach this point based on superficialities: your appearance, demeanor, and some innocuous, hopefully interesting, conversation.

This could involve successfully approaching the first woman who interests you, or the hundred and first. But I guarantee you will reach this point. Whether you succeed on the first try or only after many tries is the law of averages. Some women are available to you, others aren't. It's difficult to tell just by looking. You will get better at it over time, so if you do have a rocky beginning just take it in stride. Approach, if no positive response, move on, just be light, relaxed, conversational, pleasant, polite, assertive, modest and confident.

(At times, women who initially rebuffed you will approach you at a later occasion because they regret that they reflexively acted defensively when you approached them, and they want to at least find out a little about you and what you want before they decide. When this happens you're already a step ahead, so just take it from there.)

The immediate next step after successful introduction, in developing a relationship, is something you want to do in common. As simple as a cup of coffee, lunch, a walk in the park, a bicycle ride, tennis game, walking her home, a date for dinner. Something that interests her and that she wants to do. Preferably derived from some interest she expressed. For example you mention a new West African style restaurant that opened that people say is very good, that she expresses an interest in trying.

Obviously the more she wants to do it and the less the commitment the more likely you are to get her to accept your invitation.

If your initial conversation seems to be going well but your invitation is declined take it in stride, be polite, something like: "Maybe another time". Don't waste any more time. Move on to someone else.

If you haven't been successful with women, up to now, don't expect 100% success immediately just because you now know what you're doing. It takes practice to master technique, and the technique of approaching women, establishing rapport, and getting invitations for dates routinely accepted, is no exception.

If you're following The Principles your invitations will be accepted more and more frequently as you gain experience. Or, you may be quite happy with the first woman who accepts your invitation and stop your search right there. It's your, and her, choice.

From The Superficial To The Substantive

So we're now up to the first date.

This is the end of the beginning.

You have successfully mastered the approach, and your invitation to spend time with you has been accepted.

Now what?

We're going to discuss substantive qualities you need, and either have, or must develop.

This is where knowing what women want in a man is critical. She finds you attractive and desirable, and you made your approach the right way, so she's interested. But whether she wants a relationship with you, or not, isn't clear to her yet. And whether you want a relationship with her isn't clear to you either.

Presumably she's attractive to you or you wouldn't have approached her. But that's just as superficial an attraction you have to her, as hers is to you, at this first date stage.

What you want in a woman is entirely up to you.

But what do women want in a man they want to have a relationship with?

We now move below the superficial image to inner substance.

Women are attracted to men they perceive as having seven qualities:

1.Being a good protector.

The better the protector you are of her the more desirable you are. This is an inherent female desire. She could live in the safest environment in the world, and she will still be attracted to the good protector.

2.Being a good provider.

The better you can provide for her, presently or potentially, the more desirable you are. This is relative: To a woman with nothing a man with a $10 an hour job is a good provider. To a woman whose goal is to be kept in a luxurious style, (think: private jet, penthouse apartment in Manhattan, ski lodge in Aspen, beach house in South Hampton, maid, private chef, couture clothes, limo with driver, 'charity' galas, etc.) a man with $10 million does not have enough.

3.Being nurturing, supportive, considerate, understanding, and loyal to her.

These are personal qualities that a woman needs to form an emotional bond to a man. A man who has great sex with a woman, takes excellent care of her, protects her in every situation, and fulfills all her material desires, without creating an emotional connection, will have a transactional relationship with her, not a romance. Many men do, usually because the man is a high power, mega rich, business executive and the woman is glamorous, chic, elegant, and provides the stunning side kick and social entrée he would never otherwise have (think: Met Gala, charity balls, high level receptions, ballet openings, etc). You could set up a situation like this for yourself, if you're rich enough, but, would you want to?

4.Being on her intellectual level.

If you're on the same level you'll communicate, understand each other, share each other's thoughts even before you express them, you'll share values and opinions, see the world the same way, appreciate each other, and enjoy talking to each other. Your romance will add an intellectual level, in addition to the physical, and the emotional.

If you're considerably more intelligent than the woman, she won't consider you smart, because she isn't intelligent enough to know what intelligence is. She'll consider you odd, out of touch, that you don't make sense-which you won't - to her, that you don't know what you're talking about-because she won't understand what you're talking about. And you won't be able to have an intelligent conversation with her, because she's not capable of it. She won't want to associate with intelligent friends of yours because she won't fit in, she'll be bored, and she'll feel the same way about them as she feels about you. But she'll like and feel comfortable with her low I.Q. friends.

On the other hand if she is considerably more intelligent than you, she will lose all respect for you, pity you, denigrate any value you ever had to her, you'll bore her, and she won't communicate with you simply because you can't understand her, so why should she bother? She'll want to communicate with others on her level and that won't include you.

Either situation is miserable.

5.Being of good character.

You have to either possess good character, which women value highly, or, like most men who are successful with women, appear to have good character, but don't (women aren't all that hard to fool in this regard). Good character is quite simply being honest, never cheating, lying, or defrauding; being trustworthy; being good for your word; living up to commitments you take on; taking responsibility for the consequences of your actions; being courageous; doing your best; doing the right thing, or, if you don't have good character pretending that you do. I don't advise you to pretend to a character you don't have, but honestly, whether you have a good character, or don't, but project that you do, doesn't matter when it comes to romance. Either works;

6.Being personable.

This is just being easy to be with, being a good companion, being a good escort, being attentive, being considerate, being thoughtful, being positive, being communicative, being interested in her, in her interests, her desires, her conversation, being supportive, being interesting and adventurous to her, surprising her, exciting her, gently leading her and controlling the situation, playing the manly role and letting her play the feminine role.

7.Being desirable for sex.

A fit male body is what women want.

This is the apparent genetic make up to father a strong, attractive, intelligent, healthy child that makes a man attractive for sex. This is deeply ingrained, subconscious, not conscious, desire, a feeling not a thought. Remember humanity has been at this for

200,000 years and a lot of what's in the female mind (or for that matter the male), is patterned by this long history. And it's true whether or not children are intended then, or ever. You can't change your genetic make up but you can maximize what you appear to be by being very fit.

No matter what you look like, how in, or out, of shape, there are countless women who want, and will have, sex with you if you give them the chance, because they are shorter, lighter, younger, and in equal or worse shape than you are.

But the more physically fit you make yourself, the more women who will want sex with you, the more attractive the women who want sex with you will be, and the more eager they will be.

If you are in good enough shape, and use what you learn, you will have a lot of women who not only want, but are eager for casual sex, sometimes even preferring, one single encounter.

There are men (fairly rich celebrities) who advertise that they have had sex with over 10,000 women. Unless you're both rich and famous, and you compulsively have your entourage identify and invite women for you to have sex with, it's unlikely you'll come close to them. But you, no matter what you look like, or how little money or how much anonymity you have, will have plenty of opportunities for casual sex, as long as you seek out appropriate women. But the more fit, the more money, the more celebrity, the more opportunities. Understanding that these are relative: the high school quarterback with $100 in his pocket, may not amount to much in this big world of ours, but is likely fit enough, 'rich' enough (think: a dinner date, a trip to the beach, etc.) 'celebrity' enough, to be desired as a sex partner by quite a lot of the girls in his high school. Whether you engage in casual sex or not is up to you. But it certainly isn't what we consider a romance or intimacy.

For romance and intimacy a woman wants to be sure that, in addition to being a physical match (height, weight, age), suitable to her (attire, grooming), fulfilling the seven qualities she (and all women) want in a man, that you are committed to her. When a man provides all this for a woman she will have an irresistible drive for sex.

A proviso is in order here: It's not that you want sex with her, which I'm sure you will. It's that she must want sex with you, and she will, if you give her the time and provide the right circumstances. Also, normally, you should carefully set up the situation, then move forward as if it's spontaneous. Keep in mind that she wants sex more than you do. The drive is in her innermost female make up. So if you've laid the groundwork by demonstrating the seven qualities, you should have easy sailing.

But you should be aware that sex drive in women (like men), runs the gamut from uncontrollable desire to extreme aversion. But most women (like most men), are on a continuum. That is, they have a latent desire for sex, which they keep under control. But with the right partner, in the right circumstances, they will want and actively seek sex.

Summary Of Seven

I want to emphasize that these seven qualities are relative to the woman who interests you.

There is no objective standard.

No one is completely deficient or completely ideal in any of the seven qualities.

Whatever you're like you're, not only, fine, you're more than fine, to many women who will find you attractive and desirable, and want to be with you, as long as you follow the Principles described.

But if you're conscious of the seven qualities and consciously work at them you'll be amazed at the response you'll get.

These seven qualities are within your control.

How much you develop each one is entirely up to you.

A man who maximizes these qualities is not only attractive and desirable to women, he is irresistible.

And you can make yourself irresistible (to the woman who is right for you).

CHAPTER 7

BEING YOURSELF

I can't emphasize enough that whatever you look like, whatever your qualities, whatever your attainments, whatever your present situation, whatever your prospects there are innumerable women who will find you attractive and desirable and will want to be with you.

The more authentic you can be, the more you represent on the outside what you are on the inside, the more you will attract the interest of women who are right for you and repel those who are not, and that's what you want.

But that's not an excuse to be a slacker. If you're not in good shape that's not who you are, it's the result of not exercising. Being skinny or fat is not inherent to a man's being. It's the result of the combination of diet and physical activity. Being well or poorly informed is not inherent. You either put in time and effort to learn what you need to know or you don't. Being well or poorly educated is not inherent to you. You either do as well and go as far in school as you can, or you don't. You either strive for excellence in your occupation or you don't. You either train and practice to excel in a sport or you don't. You either develop meaningful hobbies and interests or you don't. You're not courageous or cowardly. you make yourself what you are. You are not assertive or timid. You make yourself.

You can't change your height, your race, your ethnicity, your nationality, your basic appearance, your hair quality or color, by why would you want to?

You are you. You will play out your role in life. And no one else.

Be yourself.

So if you follow what I outlined above about who and how to approach you will succeed in attracting women who are perfect for you, guaranteed.

Remember there are women out there who want to be with you even more than you want to be with them. So give them the chance.

Interests

You now know how to identify and approach a woman who will find you attractive and desirable, how to make a good impression, establish rapport, get your first date, and demonstrate that you are not just the kind of man she desires, but the man she desires, the man who stepped out of her fantasy into her reality.

You now know how to make her eager for you to call her, for you to ask her out, for you to take her out, for you to be interested in her, for you to like her, for you to want a relationship with her, for you to fall in love with her.

Now you need to concentrate on how, where, and under what circumstances you will find women who will interest you.

This is quite simple, once you get the idea.

Of course, you can meet women anywhere, in the elevator of your building, shopping in a store, at the bus stop, at work, in church, etc. Just a few casual polite words will either elicit a positive response or they won't. i.e."Did you hear the weather report for the afternoon?"; "Is the water being turned off for repairs again this afternoon?"; "Can I get something from the top shelf for you?"

Besides being haphazard, meeting women at unexpected times and places can be difficult for some men. But it will get easier for you as you gain experience. But even if you get a positive response and you make headway with a woman you meet in this way, if she isn't a match for you, don't get carried away, because you're not going anywhere with her, and it will end badly, sooner, if you're lucky, or later, if you're not.

But you can maximize your opportunities to meet women who you find attractive and desirable and who will find you attractive and desirable.

You do this by pursuing your interests as fully as you can.

If you like hiking, or camping, or cross country or downhill skiing, rock climbing, surfing, sailing, bike riding, running, tennis, golf, softball, volleyball, traveling, photography, writing, fine arts, church going, playing chess, volunteering for a good cause, etc., invest your time, effort, and attention where your interests lie. You'll find plenty of like minded women who are interested in anything and everything that interests you, and you'll find them out there doing these things.

Pursuing your interest in things like movies, music, social media, celebrities, sports, weather, places to go, things to do, that is, whatever might interest you, and what's important to your life, will also interest many women.

When you develop your abilities in things like chess, debating, crossword puzzles, foreign languages, that is, whatever interests you you'll find many women share any interest you could possibly have, and are eager to share the experience with you.

Anything you can imagine has groups centered around them, whether it's a chess club, ski club, running club, poetry society, writers' group, book club, etc. So you can always find one if you look.

Any team sport, baseball, softball, basketball, soccer, volleyball, are all valuable, but these are limited to those who are able and have the opportunity. Needless to say coed leagues are excellent places to meet fit positive women.

It doesn't matter what your interests are, as long as they're energy building, you look forward to doing them, you enjoy them, and you find them worthwhile. You'll have a richer, more fulfilling life when you give expression to your interests, and that will make you more desirable to a woman.

So figure out what you like to think about, what you like to spend your time doing, what you find worthwhile and energy building, and find a way to get involved in those things in groups, even if you form your own group.

You want to do these things in classes, teams, leagues, clubs, or groups, not alone, which could be isolating, and would likely not lead to romance.

Think outside the box. If you can imagine it, you can do it. And don't limit yourself.

Say you're interested in making movies. You can write, produce, direct, crew, act in, and edit independent movies wherever you are. With inexpensive yet high quality video, audio, and editing equipment anyone can produce and direct a movie if they want to, wherever they are.

Another suggestion is to start a non profit to address a cause you care about. It's easy and inexpensive to organize and register a non profit, and it costs little or nothing to keep it. And it can address anything from providing after school tutoring, to block parties, to conducting festivals celebrating whatever you want to celebrate, or whatever cause you want, local, national, international.

So think of whatever it is that interests you, and find a way to do it, from the simplest run in the park, to the most complicated.

Just a word of caution: make your scope as wide as you can master, but no wider. Think through whatever you have in mind from start to finish before you start it, to be sure you have at least some realistic idea of what you're getting yourself involved in.

Say, in the movie idea, others will be involved as cast and crew, and they'll be depending on you to successfully complete the best movie you can make. If you sign up for a chess tournament at a club you join you'll be expected to show up and play your best, others will be counting on you. If you join a rock climbing group on a rock climb they'll be counting on you, so be sure of what you're getting involved in. But if you are, go ahead.

Undertaking something that is important and worthwhile to you, and then pursuing it diligently and effectively is the kind of thing that makes you irresistible to women who share your interests and your passions.

They will like you and you will like them.

The activity attracts certain women, and repels others, which is a good thing.

A woman in a chess club is likely to be intellectually gifted, and if you're interested in chess you're likely intellectually gifted as well, so if all other things line up you two should be a good match.

A woman in a gym is likely to be invested in her size, strength, shape, flexibility, coordination, endurance, and if you're interested in the gym environment you probably share her interest in physical development, so again, if all other things align you should be a good match.

Of course chess players could also be gym rats but it's not common.

In the event of a perfect alignment you should definitely pursue the opportunity if the woman interests you.

Of course individual preferences come into play. On paper, you're a perfect couple, but she may, or may not, want to have a romantic relationship with you.

There are just so many influences that dictate individual preferences there is no sure way of predicting them.

There are clues. Say, a woman in your bicycle club rides as fast and as long a distance as she possibly can, you can safely assume she's competitive, that's she's not terribly sensitive, that she's driven, demands extreme effort of herself and others, and is extremely physical. But all this could be totally wrong. The only real fact is that she has strength, endurance, and some compelling drive to ride fast and far.

Make it a point to talk to each of the women, at an appropriate time, in appropriate circumstances, about an appropriate topic, whether or not they're a match for you. Just be casual, friendly, keep it light, and be responsive to each woman's signals, to either proceed to get better acquainted, keep up casual conversation when circumstances bring you together, or stay away altogether. Always keep in mind that your reputation among all the women effect how each individual woman feels about you. You're way ahead in the game If the women think you're a gentleman, that you're very nice, that you're considerate, friendly, and supportive. If any of the women interest you, are available, and they're suitable for you, by all means, try for her. After all, she's right for you and she shares an important interest of yours.

Also bear in mind that just because a woman shares an interest of yours doesn't mean The Principles of Romance don't apply. They do. Example: you enjoy the company of a woman in your bike club, and she enjoys your company, you enjoy riding with her and she enjoys riding with you, but she's not a match for you, (height, weight, age, etc.) you have a friend, but you don't have a romantic partner.

If you do get a date with a woman you meet at some activity that's it for that group, at least while you're seeing that one. Women don't like it if they're aware that you're seeing anyone other than her. It's easy to understand why. Even though it's early on, and neither of you has made any commitment. It's because of both your perceived lack of sincerity and your diminished prospect of providing the seven qualities to her.

Two cautions:

Be very careful not to volunteer for anything you're not completely sure you can accomplish.

Be sure if you take on an obligation you fulfill it.

Performing Well

People in general, and women in particular, are shallow.

Assuming there is a Judgment Day. Whether your soul is judged worthy or unworthy will surely not depend on how well you played golf or tennis, or anything else for that matter.

But how well you perform is critically important to women.

If you invite a woman who likes golf to play golf, you better, at least, play better than she does, and preferably you should play an excellent game, far superior to hers. Of course be modest and gracious, i.e. "If you were my size you would hit like me also, probably further considering you're two thirds my size and hit about eighty percent as far as me." "I played on my high school and college golf teams. If you got the kind of coaching, training and practice time I did I'm sure you'd play better than me." "I got six of the most incredible lucky bounces I've ever seen. I could never have planned them. I did nothing to land on the green six times. It just happened." etc.

That's true in everything.

The Principle is perform, at least, better than she does, or don't do the activity with her.

If the activity is important to her, and she does it better than you, she'll lose respect for you, she'll think you're not suitable for her, she won't like you, and she'll look for someone else. All very simple to avoid: "Thank you for inviting me, but golf isn't my game. I don't like to play, I don't want to spend my time on the course. I don't mind anyone who likes to play. I know a lot of people do. Including you. Everyone has their own interests and golf isn't mine. While you're playing golf, I'm going to (fill in..................) i.e. "work on the book I'm writing"/"take my kayak out"/"go rock climbing"/etc.

If she like golf, and she plays better than you, invite her to go sailing on your boat, if you can handle the boat better than she can. Or to go skiing, if you ski better than she does. Just don't play golf with her.

If playing golf with her is crucial to her, and you don't want to find someone else, you can take lessons, practice, gain experience, and become better than her. If you can become better you can play golf with her but if you can't, you're in a lose-lose situation.

The more knowledgeable, the more experienced, the more skillful, the better the performer, in whatever interest you choose to pursue, the more desirable you will be to women who share your interest. This is an example of how women's shallowness helps you. You're not a better person because you won a chess tournament, or a running race, or whatever. But she'll think you are.

Fact: If you perform better than her she'll think more of you, if you perform worse than her she'll think less of you.

CHAPTER 8

TIME TOGETHER

You have identified, approached, and successfully introduced yourself to a woman who is, at least, superficially perfect for you. Height, weight, age, fitness, attire, grooming, you elicit a nice, welcoming response to your facial expression, nice smile, eye contact, body language, tone of voice, confidence, assertiveness, obvious strength and gentleness, and conversation. She finds you attractive and desirable and you've won enough trust that she wants to spend time with you, and get to know you better.

This is where you want to be. Everything that came before was to get you to this point. Now you're here.

You ask for her number, you call promptly, that same day, and you start dating.

As you develop your relationship, you must invest time, effort, and thought, without being intrusive.

A woman assumes that if you don't call you're not thinking of her and you're not interested. So if you don't call because you're shy or you're afraid you'll be turned down, your just being foolish. The term here is 'Man up'. Be a man. Take a chance. If you're turned down, move on. Women like to be asked out. If you choose who you call according to what I explained to you, the woman you call will find you attractive and desirable, and she'll be flattered by your attention.

If you don't spend time with her she'll look for others to spend time with.

So, immediately begin to invite without being intrusive. If you're not sure call immediately but allow about one week notice. Your first date should be relatively simple and close to her home, unless you specifically discussed say, going hiking, skiing, or sailing together. The 'normal' first date is for dinner close to home. Be sure you make a reservation, and if you invite for a specific place and you have to take her somewhere else let her know in advance.

There are important things to know about being in a woman's company.

Strength And Gentleness

Women desire men who they perceive as strong and gentle. You can demonstrate strength (without showing off or being obvious about it) but always be gentle with her. This combination is irresistible to women.

The Male Role

Whatever a feminist might say, you must, and women want you to, play the male role and women want to play the female role. The male role in a relationship is to be in control of the situation and show leadership, in a gentle, thoughtful, considerate, respectful (not worshipful or submissive), way. This is the opposite of any degree of force, compulsion, threat, or harm, which is never acceptable in any circumstance or in any situation.

The woman always has the ultimate say in what she wants, and her desire must be fulfilled without hesitation or complaint. If she doesn't want to go somewhere or do something she doesn't go there or do it, if she wants to go home that's exactly where you take her when she wants to be taken there. Your control and leadership must be used to control the situation and to lead her where she wants to go, no where else. But she will want to go where you want to take her if you play your role properly, that is to plan ahead, to know what you're doing, to be thoughtful, and considerate of her, her thoughts, her feelings, her needs, her capabilities, her desires, even her fears, anxieties, or reluctance.

Women want you to be in control and to lead them, it's inherent to the female mind, as long as you do so in the proper spirit.

She has to know that you will always have her best interests at heart, will always be considerate, always thoughtful, always protective, and that, ultimately, you will do what she asks of you, so that she feels safe and secure in your company. Nothing less is acceptable from you at any time.

You will display strength and gentleness, confidence, assertiveness and manliness, by your conduct and demeanor. You show these qualities, you don't talk about these qualities.

She must come to trust in you herself by the image you project, and reality you create.

Either you have these attributes now, or you will develop these attributes, which are critical to romance.

Exclusive Attention

From the time you arrive to pick up your date to the time that you leave her you give her your exclusive attention.

Don't take or make any calls, don't talk on your phone, don't send or look at any texts; don't look at any other women.

During that time she is the only woman in the world who means anything to you.

Competence

Be politely assertive and decisive in handling whatever comes up. If you make a mistake take it in stride. Have a good sense of humor.

Get as much knowledge as you can about what you're going to do. For example where is the theater? How do you get there from your date's apartment? Are you going by ride hailing service? Which one? If you can, try the app on your phone before your date so you know it works and how to do it.

But if you do have a problem, and you will if you date enough, which you probably will, just take it in stride. As I recommend, always have a Plan B in mind just in case what you're planning doesn't work out. But don't get flustered. If a restaurant doesn't find your reservation, or you went somewhere without a reservation and they're hugely crowded, and you don't have a Plan B, or Plan B doesn't work out, be calm, discuss what to do, and do something plausible.

Remember, she accepted a date with you to have a nice time in your company. The theater, restaurant, baseball game, hot air balloon ride, or whatever, nice as they might have been, are not the main thing. So if you turn a night at the theater into bowling, or dinner at a certain restaurant into an interesting food court, or a baseball game into picnic in the park, and your balloon ride into a trip to a nearby botanic garden, and a nice lunch there, and you're with a woman who's right for you, it should not only be ok, it should be more than ok.

How you handle adversity, unexpected events, challenges, obstacles, and problems is the essence of competence.

If you don't handle something well, or it's your 'fault' that things didn't work out as you planned, possibly because of inexperience, and you can't straighten it out, it's not critical, as long as you're calm, in control, don't get flustered, take it in stride, and do something plausible, with a good sense of humor.

If you don't get another date with the woman you were with she wasn't right for you anyway. No one wants a 'fair weather friend', and you don't want a relationship with a 'fair weather' woman who's going to desert you when (not if) the going gets tough for you, because in life, you will have patches of rough going, unless you play it so safe you've already let rough patches defeat you. And if you were that type of person you wouldn't be reading this book.

Conversation With Your Date

You must be prepared to go into a lot more depth and breadth than you did when you first spoke to a woman who accepted a date with you.

People who are relaxed and spontaneous in conversation are the most prepared.

There's nothing wrong with taking notes (in private), reviewing them before meeting, and discussing things you made notes on in an interesting way. Normally you create a pattern in your mind, and visualize it, so you can remember your list when you can't look at it. Just don't let anyone know you do this. So you can't bring your notes with you, nor can you leave them where they could be found.

Also, don't be rigid. Pick up on anything that's brought up, and explore anything your date brings up. Only return to your list of memorized topics if there's a lapse in conversation.

As an example of advance preparation: suppose you are going on a date to see a specific movie the woman who interests you wants to see, which has a star who interests her.

You can look up quite a bit of information about the movie, say, where it was filmed, how long it took to film, its budget, what countries it's most popular in, perhaps something interesting that happened during the filming. Same with the star. Perhaps where she was born, her parents' occupations, how she got her start, what she was paid to be in the movie.

What you discuss has to be what interests your date.

If you bring up the budget and the pay and she's not interested in this aspect she's liable to say: "Everything is about money to you. Don't you care about anything else?". So be careful of what you bring up. Also, if she says: "How do you know so much about the movie and the star?" there's nothing wrong with saying you were curious and you looked it up. There is something very wrong with saying that you looked it up to have something to talk to her about-that makes it sound like you have nothing in common, that you're a manipulative phony. The purpose of preparation is to seem spontaneous. There's nothing wrong with looking some-thing up because you're interested in it and there's nothing wrong with sharing what you learned. There's a fine line, don't cross it.

A few more suggestions:

You're going to a botanic garden: read about it, pick out some interesting details, and be ready to mention them especially if there's a lull in the conversation. You can even say: "I was curi-ous about the garden so I looked up a few things about it", then discuss.

You're going to play tennis: Look up how the dimensions of the court came about, or the rules, or the scoring system.

You're going on a hike: Look up the geography, geology, wildlife, birds, and history of the area, legends, myths, etc.

You get the idea. The possibilities are endless. Tie them into the interests of the woman you are taking, if she's interested in flowers, art, science, history, movies, that's where you direct your preparation.

The objective is not to have any awkward silence. If conversation is going smoothly obviously don't derail the natural flow just because you spent an hour looking up, outlining, committing to memory, and figuring out an interesting way to present something.

Always remember, your objective is to be good company, entertaining, interesting, engaging.

If you continue dating what you discuss should include more personal topics or your relationship will not progress.

But you have to get there step by step. Give her a chance to express herself. Then be attentive, sympathetic, and supportive.

Anything she tells you about herself is an invaluable opening. Be sure to take advantage of the opportunity to be interested, to be supportive, to be on her side. But don't be a phony. There's nothing wrong with saying "I'm not sure that you handled that in the best way possible (especially if she knows that already), but I understand why you did, and I probably would have done the same thing."

If you tell her about yourself, be sure it's positive, and be sure it puts you in a good light.

She might say something like: "Tell me something about yourself I don't know now, but I'll find out later, but I would want to know now" So you might say, "I try to work at least some time every single day. Sometimes just an hour or so at home but every day, even holidays. I just want to be the best at what I do. Know more than anyone else. I know it's probably not possible, but I want to be the best in the world at what I do."

Be Appreciative

You should definitely end your date with a sincere complement.

For example: you disregarded my advise and argued with your

date. Don't leave it at that. You say: "I realize how strongly you feel about that, and I understand why you said what you said, you made good points, and you supported them well." You might say: "I have to think about what you said. I really felt I was right, but I think maybe I have to rethink the entire thing." or: "I respect your position. I'm sorry I argued with you. You're entitled to an opinion and we don't have to agree on everything. I respect that you feel strongly about what you're saying. On this I think I have to say 'we have to agree to disagree on this' but I recognize that there can be more than one take on this. And I would like to say I like the way you stand your ground. When you believe you're right you stand up for it, and I like that about you."

I wouldn't let your date depart your company with any residual negative feeling if you can not only defuse it but turn it to your advantage, as in the argument example instead of her departing your company angry and frustrated at how wrong and stubborn you are, she leaves feeling good about herself and you because you express your admiration for the way she stood up for what she believes with courage and skill.

More likely your date was entirely positive. You listened to her with interest and respect and you had a very nice time. But you still end with some sincere complement.

But it must be honest and sincere.

Example: You're at a restaurant and a bunch of glamorous models come in and create a big stir, and attract a lot of men, and a big scene develops around them, and she feels very uncomfortable, and maybe a little down on herself. Don't just tell her she was the most beautiful woman there. But you can tell her: "You are a beautiful person inside and out, I've never met someone who's so much in every way. And I don't think I ever will. So I can say something: 'you were the most beautiful woman in that place tonight'."

"You made watching that tennis match so much more interesting, I had no idea you knew so much about tennis strategy"

"You're take on the motivation of the characters in the movie is brilliant. I would have said the movie was kind of okay, but now, after hearing what you said I think that movie is one of the best I ever saw. Actually I want to see it again, and really appreciate it more. You should write a column on film. People would love it. I should take you to every movie I see."

Even: "It was very nice spending the evening with you."

Bottom line: Be honest, be appreciative of her and her company and tell her so, but find something positive in even the worst circumstances.

Let's say she was complaining the whole time: "It's too hot, the sun is too strong, this umbrella is terrible, this lounge is uncomfortable, the cushion is too thin, it's too crowded, the food is terrible, those were the worst drinks I ever had, the water is too cold, and the surf is too rough there, I hate that beach, I'm never going back there" But you could say: "I could say all the same things, but, the sight of you in that bathing suit more than made up for everything else. I couldn't take my eyes off you. You always look beautiful, but today, on that beach, you looked absolutely incredible. I will always remember the way you looked today on that beach."

CHAPTER 9

There are no real rules governing when and how to start and make progress on intimacies.

Women usually want intimacy, but most women not only won't make the first move, they won't make any move. No matter how much they want a romantic relationship with you, women will leave it to you to take the initiative.

Just advance gently and slowly enough so that if she wants to back away she can.

If she's not ready than nothing happens.

Never be aggressive or apply even the slightest pressure.

You have to take the initiative, but she has to go along. If she doesn't you have a friend perhaps, and that's good, but you'll have to look elsewhere for a romantic relationship.

It's certainly not pressuring to say "I have to find someone who feels about me the way I feel about her." as opposed to simply not calling her anymore. If she decides to have a romantic relationship with you that's her choice. If she chooses to stop seeing you that's her choice, or your joint choice, also.

Normally if you are dating a woman she expects romance and intimacy and if you don't provide it she will look elsewhere.

A relationship can't stay still. It has to move forward, or it sinks.

If either or both don't want a romantic relationship, come to an understanding that you will either be friends or stop seeing each other. And, while it's nice to have a female friend, it does complicate things for you. But either way, if the situation doesn't develop into a romance than you have to find someone else.

Be Active Not Passive

If things go well, you should follow up by calling promptly, say the next day. If you don't call promptly, she'll assume you're not interested, and may accept a date with someone else when she wanted you. Also, if you wait, say until Wednesday for a Saturday date, she's liable to think you called her only because others turned you down, and that she's not your first choice.

But if your first date goes well, and she accepts your invitation for a second, you're on the right path, but you need to get creative.

If you don't organize activities that she's interested in, she'll look for activities to get involved in that do interest her.

So don't plan on a string of 100 dinner dates.

Put in effort to plan and organize activities you'll both enjoy, then invite her with a well thought through presentation.

Ideally you combine her interests and desires with yours. If you can, and do, you're off.

What you plan, invite for, and carry out starts simple and becomes involved, walk in the park, tennis game, scuba diving, sailing, hot air balloon, ski week end, week in the caribbean, two weeks in Europe, summer rental by the beach, etc. Try to make them as exciting, adventurous, and surprising as you can. But always things she will look forward to and enjoy. First, both of you have a great time. Second you have her thinking: "What's next with this guy?" To succeed in this she has to feel safe and secure in your company, so be sure that she is, and that she knows that she is.

Only your imagination, time, finances, and ability limits you. But whatever you can provide will be exciting to some women but inadequate to others.

In the event that she asks you to take her somewhere you should, and do it graciously. She's asking you because it's important to her to go there and she wants you to be the one who takes her. Don't let her down.

Some cautions:

As I mentioned, be good at whatever it is you invite for. Women have respect for men who do things better than they do. As an example if you invite for tennis be sure you're a better player than she is or don't play tennis with her. If you invite for scuba diving be sure you can do it, do it well, and do it better than she can. Bottom line: you should have more knowledge and more skill in anything you do together.

Plan well so things go well. Whenever possible, and it should always be possible, have a Plan B so if things don't work out the way you planned you can do something else. Say, for example, you drive out somewhere for a hot air balloon ride but the weather turns bad and you can't go. Have something else in the area you can suggest so the day isn't a complete failure.

Ignore feminist tripe about 'equality'. Regardless of relative finances you will ordinarily be expected to pay the entire cost of anything you do. If the woman offers to contribute you should politely decline. This means you have to limit yourself to what you can afford. If you can't afford her, the earlier you find that out the better.

If a woman's not satisfied with what you can provide, don't go into hock trying. When you can't borrow any more she'll drop you anyway, and you'll owe money you can't afford to repay.

You'll be financially crippled in your search for romance and she'll be on to the next guy. Get a woman in your price range.

If you don't share any interests and there's nothing you both like to do, (which doesn't mean doing everything together all the time, which no one should want anyway) you're probably not right for each other anyway. Even if you could sustain a relationship based on all the other criteria, you would probably wind up living completely separate lives, with completely separate friends, completely different interests and values, and less and less in common. So why would you want that when there are so many other women you could share your life with, which also means she would be sharing her life with you?

Another proviso, she 'owes' you nothing except her company. After a hugely expensive elegant dinner out she wants to be taken directly to her home that's exactly where she gets taken. If she doesn't want a kiss goodnight that's exactly what she doesn't get. If she doesn't want to be walked to her door that's exactly where you don't walk her to. You say goodnight in a pleasant and polite way. You wait, where you are, until she's safely inside, and you leave.

But remember, it's not always about you. Maybe she feels terribly sick, or nauseous, or needs the bathroom very badly and doesn't want the restaurant bathroom, or has an unbearable migraine headache, or feels like she's going to pass out, or has, what is to her, some embarrassing, unexpected female emergency, or any one of 1,000 reasons, that she doesn't want to explain to you at the moment.

On the other hand it's possible you inadvertently said or did something that's a 'Deal Breaker'. A 'Deal Breaker' is anything a particular woman finds so repulsive she can't or won't have anything more to do with you. So it could be about you.

You call her the next day, which you should just to check that she's all right. She may, or may not, tell you what the problem was. It's alright to ask: "Did I do something wrong?" But if she doesn't want to discuss it, drop it.

You can ask for another date, if you wish, and you'll quickly find out if it's you and it's over, or if it was some other unspecified reason.

If it was you, try to understand what you said or did, learn from your mistake, move on, but don't repeat because you'll likely get the same reaction.

Example of a "Deal Breaker": Her dad has told her how his life was saved while he was on combat duty in the army by a courageous sergeant, who now lives on the other side of the country. He calls to say hello because he's in the neighborhood on business, so her dad invites him over for dinner. The door opens and the sergeant is of another race. They have a wonderful dinner and visit and part in the warmest most affectionate way. On your first date, say, one night later, you make some stupid, thoughtless, ignorant, insulting racist comment. She doesn't change expression or make comment and the moment passes. But that was the "Deal Breaker", from which there's no coming back.

Of course I recommend that you never make any stupid, thoughtless, ignorant, insulting comments about anything, ever. For purposes of what I'm explaining to you it's poor practice. But how you conduct yourself is up to you.

Now let's get back to the positive.

First dates go well. You both want more of each other's company.

Deepening Your Relationship

There is a proven way to develop a relationship of romance and intimacy.

This is governed by Principles just like every other aspect of romance.

In the short term personality is key. She likes being with you, she like your conversation, she likes the way you handle what comes up, she feels safe and secure with you, she feels cared for, respected and valued, she believes you take her needs and desires into consideration, that you're always thoughtful and considerate, she looks forward to your calls, and to your time together.

But usually no real issues of life comes up during the dating phase of a relationship. Even if you live together for a while.

Personality remains important, and you need to keep up what got you to this point, but it's not the key to a successful long term relationship.

In the long term, character is key.

Character is shown by conduct:

You're a slacker. You avoid responsibility. You waste money on things you can't afford and don't need. You're not there when you're needed. You're not reliable. You're inconsiderate. You're selfish. You don't pull your weight. You shirk responsibility. You don't do your best. You avoid obligations. You take advantage of her. You're dishonest. You're a cheat, a fraud and a thief.

Or, you prove your worth with honesty and integrity, you try hard, and do your best in every situation. You do whatever you have to do to uphold your duties and obligations.

Caution: A man of high character can succumb to allowing his relationship with a woman to become 'transactional' rather than a real relationship of romance, intimacy, and sex.

A 'transactional' relationship is one in which each side does what's required, period. Say, the man becomes, or is, very rich, and provides a luxurious lifestyle, and the woman becomes a glamorous, elegant, chic, trophy wife, who gains the couple social acceptance among rich people. They could also have a loving relationship, and there's no reason why they couldn't. Except that if the woman's criteria was a rich man, and the man's criteria was stunning beauty, with elegance, and social graces, it's unlikely, since 'human' qualities were factored out. But it's not impossible if they both try.

A relationship requires time. You may work long hours, you may want time in the gym, or golf course, or whatever, but if you don't carve out time the woman you care about will look to fill her own time, in her own way, which won't include you.

To avoid this you need to invest time, effort, thought, and resources into providing all the qualities the woman you are in a relationship with desires. You plan surprises, interesting adventures, things she wants to do; you demonstrate thoughtfulness with personal gifts, gestures; you take the time and attention to listen to her, her interests, concerns, hopes, dreams, anxieties, and fears; you prove to be supportive and sympathetic; she knows she always has an ally to take her side, a friend who will always be with her, a confidante whom she can trust, someone totally trustworthy, someone she is very lucky to have found and joined up with, and in these ways you sustain a relationship of romance, intimacy, and sex.

All of life is priority, and you have to decide what is yours

CHAPTER 10

EMPATHY

To truly take charge you must see through the woman's eyes, think her thoughts, detect her world view, her level of intelligence, understand her values, know what's important to her, sense her hopes and dreams, her anxieties and fears, and discern what moves her.

When you are a master of empathy you know the woman better than she knows herself.

You know how she's going to react to whatever it is she encounters before she encounters it, you know what she's going to think before she thinks it, you know what she's going to feel before she feels it, you know what she's going to want to do before she knows what she wants to do.

You don't use empathy to become her, you are always yourself, and you must play the male role in the relationship. You use empathy solely as a tool.

When you are good at this you control the situation, and manipulate her thoughts, feelings, and behavior, essentially any way you want, as long as you present the stimulus properly and handle her the way she wants to be handled.

You can take her anywhere you want to go, but you have to make her want to go there, and you must take her there the way she wants to get there.

Every woman wants to be treated in a certain way, patterned by her past experience, her self image, and her circumstances.

You can either treat her that way or find someone else.

Although you control a woman's thoughts and feelings and you control her behavior she won't know you're doing it, because you make her want to think, feel, and do whatever you want her to. She wants to spend the night in your apartment, she wants to go away for the weekend with you, she wants to go for a swim with you at a deserted beach. You just have to make her come to it on her own.

It's not that you want her to do these things, it's that she wants to do these things, and she knows you'll want to and you'll go along with her.

Some men are naturally good at this, others haven't a clue, and most are somewhere along the spectrum.

You can succeed without having any empathy at all because all women want a man who is taller, heavier, older, more sophisticated, more educated, higher in status, higher earning, wealthier, more athletic, fit, strong, healthy, energetic, assertive, decisive, strong, gentle, considerate, thoughtful, attentive, supportive, and appreciative of her (without being worshipful), a good protector and a good provider.

If you're a physician and you meet a woman who's wants to marry a physician, your rich and you meet a woman who wants to marry a rich man, your a man in society and you meet a woman who wants to be in this society, and especially if you meet all the other criteria you will succeed with her, whether you understand the first thing about her or not, but she'll pick you, you won't pick her, and she'll control you, you won't control her. There are workable relationships that follow this pattern, and if you're ok with this then it's ok for you. But you'll be a lot happier and more fulfilled if you have more control over your life.

You learn about her by gaining her trust, by never telling anyone anything she tells you, by keeping her secrets no matter what, by taking her side-even if you think she is wrong about something, by being supportive, by taking an interest in what concerns her, by doing your best to try to understand her world view, her understanding of things, her values. To do this you have to focus your attention on her.

Remember that how a person says something, their tone of voice, facial expressions, body language, as well as what they choose to talk about, and not talk about, are all equally important.

Always converse as an equal, never interrogate, never humor, never be sarcastic, never be didactic, never lecture, never criticize, listen more than you talk, be sure you understand what she is saying, and if you're attentive you should be able to determine her level of intelligence and understanding, her values, what she finds interesting and what she doesn't find interesting, what qualities she likes and what qualities she doesn't like, how she likes to be treated, what she wants to do, where she wants to go, how she sees herself, and how she sees you.

Ordinarily your attitude toward a woman is that you like her just the way she is, that you see nothing wrong, and whatever she may think of herself that is less than flattering you do not agree with. For example, if she confides in you that she thinks she has fat legs your response is that you think she has very nice legs.
But be sincere. If she thinks you are not being honest you will break the bond of trust that is vital to a romantic relationship.

Women naturally seek to detect lack of sincerity. Many men have an even greater ability to project an image of sincerity, they don't have, that consistently evades women's detection. But if you don't, and many men don't, simply be honest, yet discrete. If you stupidly agree that she has fat legs and should, say, follow up on her idea to diet and exercise, you'll probably never see her again. You might try "You're a certain kind of woman, and you're beautiful in your own way. I think you're beautiful just as you are."

Hopefully you're being honest, and if you're not perhaps you should move on. And if you are being sincere, and you convey that sincerity convincingly, you will very likely make headway.

As you begin to learn, and to employ, empathy, you begin to wield a powerful tool. You may be very successful, and even surprise yourself with what you accomplish. The power to evoke interest in you, love, desire, eagerness to be with you, to deepen her relationship with you, to please you, to make you happy, to do what you want, is a great power to have over someone.

But you may, at times, err, and evoke the opposite response to what you were trying for. Nearly everyone makes mistakes at times. Sometimes due to a woman's inner conflict, contradiction, lack of insight, or even dishonesty with herself or with you, that you didn't detect. If you evoke a negative response, you may or may not be able to undo it. If you can't, chalk it up to a learning experience, minimize the damage-you don't want anyone bad mouthing you behind your back, and move on.

Another problem, which you can't do much about is that a woman might tell you some secret about herself, that because you know it, might cause her not to want to have a relationship with you. It might, or might not, seem significant to you, but it might be to her. She may deeply regret having told you, perhaps in a moment of weakness, or neediness, in the protective embrace of your interest, supportiveness, and sympathy. For example, that she had been in an in-patient psychiatric facility, or had an abortion, or had sex with casting directors to get parts in movies, was gang raped as an adolescent when she lived in a trailer park, etc. Now, for knowing that you know this about her, she can't bear to be with you, no matter how understanding and supportive you are, and how dedicated you are to keeping her secret. On the other hand your handling of a revelation of this kind might cinch your relationship with her.

Just remember, when you swing for a home run with bases loaded you may strike out, or you may hit a grand slam home run.

Don't feel discouraged if you can't figure a woman out. You'll get better at it, if you try. If you're not naturally good at it, it can be a slow process. You have to feel yourself along. Talk to her about what interests her, things she's willing to share with you. Listen to her carefully. Try to understand what she's thinking and feeling. Incrementally you'll understand her better and better. You'll learn to take her part, to be her emotional partner, and she'll look forward to opening up to you, sharing with you, and having you as her partner.

CHAPTER11

UNDERSTANDING WOMEN

As you get experience with women you learn that every woman is a unique individual, but all share one quality in common when it comes to romance, intimacy, and sex.

They approach romance emotionally not intellectually. When it comes to romance women feel, they don't think.

Their emotions are governed by innate female drives, but they don't know this. They just feel the way they do.

They feel a certain way about men, not because they think them through, but because their response is ingrained and patterned.

Even if they studied psychology in college in depth, and thoroughly learned the psychology of innate female drives, they would still behave exactly the same way in their own lives.

It's not that they can't behave any differently, it's that they don't want to.

There are some women so dumb you can't believe they're being serious when they talk, all along the gamut to women who amaze you with their intellectual brilliance. Brilliant women have an incisive intelligence that blows you away in even the most mundane matters. But you won't win either one with the intellect. Smartest to stupidest you win them through their emotions, or not at all.

A woman can describe why they find a certain man (you perhaps), attractive and desirable, but whatever they say, or even think, is not why they're interested.

A woman might say about a man she's interested in: "He has a great sense of humor" but look at all the other criteria and you'll see he meets them all.

A woman is drawn to you because you are bigger, taller, older, in good physical shape, present a nice appearance, energetic, more intelligent, more sophisticated, better educated, higher earning (or potentially higher earning say, a medical student), higher status, than she is; you are strong and gentle, self confident and modest, assertive, decisive, calm, in control, considerate, thoughtful, supportive, positive; you share (or pretend to share) the same interests, values, goals, world view, you are interesting (to her), nice for her to talk to and be with; you protect and provide for her; and you're interested in her.

All of these qualities are relative. You can't be all things to all women, no man can. So, if you're not 'all things' to a woman don't give it one moments regret. Just move on. But you can be all things to some women. And it's one of those women that is your romantic partner, (or partners if you are so inclined).

If you choose the woman to direct your attention to carefully, she will find you compellingly attractive and desirable, she will be emotionally drawn to you, and, as rigid as the Principles of attraction she follows are, she won't have a clue.

She'll be eager for you to find her attractive, to have you pay attention to her, and to be her provider and protector, because she feels the desire for you deep within her being.

She may not want children, but if you have a nice body, 200,000 years of ingrained female desire compels her to want sex with you. That female drive has kept the human race going for a long time, and it's not stopping now.

Given the right circumstances with the right man it's very hard for women to hold themselves back.

Remember, she wants a man. She wants a man for romance, for intimacy, for sex. Whether you are the man she wants depends on you, not her.

The qualities you have developed and demonstrated to her, turn her on, or turn her off.

Your choice.

CHAPTER 12

Women sometimes say "Men are jerks".

That's because men who are successful with women present themselves in the way that women desire. To do this in the most successful way men completely separate the way they present themselves from the way they are. So if a man works out enough to have an ideal body, approaches women who are a perfect match, and act the part of the man of her dreams, strong and gentle, considerate, etc. it can all be an act, but it works, and a woman will surrender to him, but sooner or later who the man really is and what he wants comes out.

The second aspect, which is sort of the same but seen from the female perspective. Women demand a certain type of man, with the qualities I outline. So, a man has to project these qualities whether he has them or not. So, men who want to be successful with women are put into the position of being what a woman wants and not what he is. But again, sooner or later his true self and his real intentions come out.

The third aspect is kind of unfortunate. People tend not to value what they have a lot of. Men who are successful with women have a lot of women readily available to them. So they tend not to value them very highly, and often treat them like they're disposable, which, to them, if they're not looking for a long term relationship, they are. This is particularly true for beautiful women with great bodies who aren't too swift. Think: a beautiful, sexy, woman who is not very intelligent, not very educated, not very good at anything, not very interesting to talk to or be with, selfish, self=centered, demanding. A man comes on with an ardent approach, he's perfect for her, the man of her dreams, and he knows just how to play her, because he wants to try her out in bed. But after a few times he gets bored with her, and he's on to the next, just as beautiful, just as great a body.

A fourth aspect is that only women who meet strict criteria, i.e. shorter, lighter, younger, lower status, etc. are available even to men who are most successful with women. In fact, it's limiting themselves to women who are appropriate to them that makes them so successful. But the negative is that men who are successful with women don't even like many of the women they start a relationship with. The women have nice bodies, or exciting or entertaining sex techniques, or have some other aspect to them they want to explore. But as soon as they do, they're on to the next. Because these women are less intelligent, less able, less sophisticated, less accomplished, less personable, less interesting, so much slower, weaker, less athletic, they're just not a long term partner to the man who easily wins them over.

That is why women say: "Men are jerks".

Once you master the techniques in this book, how you conduct yourself is up to you.

I might like to say there's right or wrong in this, but there isn't, neither is there correct or incorrect, moral or immoral.

There is honesty, or at least discretion. And dishonesty-if you make promises you know you're not going to keep, or lead a woman on knowing you're not taking her where she thinks she's going with you. But even honesty and dishonesty isn't right or wrong. It's just part of romance.

In essence, a woman demands certain things to give herself to a man, and a man meets those demands in order to get the woman.

And that's it, nothing more.

So you may be, in the eyes of at least some women, one of those jerks, or maybe you will not.

If you are what women consider "a jerk" you can avoid the label by breaking up in a way that doesn't leave anger, resentment, bitterness, humiliation, a sense of being victimized. Put a little time, effort, and thought into why you can't see each other anymore so she feels good about herself, and positive about the time you spent together.

CHAPTER 13

MAXIMIZING WHAT YOU ARE

You can prepare for anything, romance included.

Don't listen to anyone who says you can't.

You will live one kind of life if you prepare yourself, and another kind if you don't.

It's your choice.

What kind of man you are is entirely up to you.

You can be a man that other men admire and women desire.

Your stature as a man is directly relevant to how desirable a romantic partner you are. Every man, no matter who, has stature in the eyes of a woman somewhere.

You could do nothing at all, and simply using the knowledge you gained already, identify and successfully pursue opportunities to find romance, intimacy, and sex, that are essentially limited only by your time, energy, interest, and means.

Whoever you are, whatever physical shape you're in, whatever your educational attainments, occupation, earnings, money, social strata, status, and reputation, that are essentially limitless female prospects that are, not only interested in you, but eager to be with you.

There is a woman for every man. If you are alone, somewhere out there, the woman who should have been with you is alone also.

If you are lonely you made her lonely.

You want a woman who's a match for you.

If you are going to form a relationship with someone who you find impressive you must make yourself into someone who is impressive, that is, her match.

If you want a woman who is feminine you must be manly, if you want a woman who is in excellent physical shape you must be in excellent physical shape, if you want a woman who is intellectually stimulating you must be intellectually stimulating, if you want a woman who is adventurous you must be adventurous, if you want a woman who is athletic you must be athletic, if you want a woman who is interesting you must be interesting, if you want a woman who is well educated you must be well educated, if you want a woman who is of high character you must have high character, if you want a woman who is personable you must be personable, if you want a woman who is nice to talk to you must be nice to talk to.

Competition

You are not the only man who fits all the criteria for a given woman who interests you, nor is she the only woman who is appropriate for you, who will find you attractive, desirable and want to be with you.

Competition runs in both directions, among men for women and among women for men.

A good place to see this in action is a typical summer camp that has, say, ten male and ten female counselors. Normally they will quickly pair off, following the Principles I described to you. But within the height, weight, age, criteria, there will be a few women and a few men who are appropriate for each other. Who winds up with who is based on who is more desirable to each other. That's where level of fitness, strength and gentleness, confidence, interests, skills, conversation, empathy, etc. come in.

If you follow The Principles of Romance you will win over many women, without doing anything to improve yourself.

But the more time, effort, and thought you put into maximizing your potential, the more you'll get out of it.

And you'll increase your competitive advantage with the result that you'll win more women, who are better looking, nicer, more personable, more desirable. You may not want a long term relationship with the best looking or sexiest woman you can win because she may (or may not be) shallow, selfish, egotistical, cold, uncaring, unintelligent, uninteresting. But it's nice to be able to have the easiest time, with the most number, of the most desirable women.

Now we will discuss what you can do to maximize your potential.

Bear in mind, there is what you can easily attain, and what you can attain.

As a general rule, and correct on a depressingly regular basis, it takes an inordinate amount of time to accomplish something, which, once you've accomplished it, you can accomplish again so quickly and easily that, thinking back, you wonder how it could possibly have taken you so much time, effort, and frustration, to achieve the first time.

I went over what you need to be concerned with. But I want to go into a little more detail to share my thoughts with you, and to be sure we understand each other.

Physical

If you're in ideal shape, just keep doing what you're doing. If you're not start a physical exercise regime immediately.

If you've been sedentary you're not going to like exercising. The body accustoms itself to whatever you accustom it to. And, if you've been sedentary you probably incline to it. So you have to countermand your natural inclination and habituation to become active. But once you accustom yourself to being physically active you'll like it, you'll look forward to it (though you'll find it hard to believe me on this when you first get started), and once you get established in your exercise regime you'll never want to live a sedentary lifestyle again, and you'll wonder why you ever did. The reason why this is true is because being active is normal and healthy for a person's body.

But I cannot emphasize enough that you must start slowly. The more sedentary you have been, the weaker you are, the more over, or under weight, the slower you must go. When you start you'll have a reserve of rested muscle capacity, but don't let that little jump start fool you into pushing yourself into discouraging exhaustion and harmful injury.

You must build muscle fiber, strengthen your tendons and ligaments, strengthen your joints, build your heart (which is a muscle), improve your circulation, and your breathing, slowly, or you'll put too much stress on your body before you're ready for it.

Use your mind and your body to guide yourself.

It's advisable to work in adequate rest days, and be careful not to overtrain to exhaustion or injury.

Daily effort is anywhere from an hour to two hours, but results depend upon effort, technique, form, intensity, and proper training regimen.

There's no easy way.

An excellent start is to do push ups beginning with as many as you can, then gradually building up. The plank is an abdominal strengthening exercise that people have excellent results with. A flat firm mid section is crucial to looking and feeling good, and being attractive to women. (It's also very healthy.) Flexibility routines are valuable, but start slowly. If you're unsure of proper form just check the internet.

As soon as possible start weight training, beginning with light weights you can handle well, and slowly building. You can buy an inexpensive set of hand weights that take additional weights as you build up. You can do your exercise right in your room very conveniently. Don't be discouraged if you can only handle a small amount of weight because you will build steadily. When you go up in weight stay at that level for a while until you feel comfortable before you go up again or you'll risk injury, and you don't want that. There's no hurry, you'll get there. Whereas if you push yourself too hard and too fast you'll injure yourself and be worse off than when you started.

Running/jogging is extremely valuable for speed, strength, endurance, fitness and health.

If you haven't done any running you must start slowly. Don't push yourself to go faster or farther than you feel comfortable. Running programs are weekly. They demand one to two rest days a week, as well as interspersed speed work and distance. You will improve rapidly in the beginning while your speed and distance lies within your already available anatomic and physiologic capabilities. But as you must build heart, lung, circulatory, muscle, tendon, ligament, and bone strength to increase speed and distance, improvement will come much more slowly. Don't rush because that predictably results in discouragement, pain, and injury (injury is not the same thing as pain). But pain is a warning of break down, so ease up if you feel pain until you can exercise pain-free. Given, at least, an average degree of good health, if you follow an intelligent, disciplined, and diligent weekly training regime, you'll improve rapidly over a few months. You'll get the health and fitness benefits right away. If you're interested in health, fitness, and appearance all you need is a 3 to 5 miles, total running time 30-60 minutes, five to six days a week.

Just to quantify, an 8-10 minute mile is very respectable for a recreational runner. But if you continue a diligent training regime with speed and endurance work, you will likely be able to do a mile in 5-7 minutes depending on how suited your anatomy and physiology is for running that distance, and how diligently you train.

Overall unless you're committed to distance running I would recommend no more than four to five miles a day, or whatever distance you feel comfortable doing, at whatever speed you feel comfortable at, without suffering pain and break down. You will get maximum benefit without risking break down, that often, but not necessarily, accompanies long distance running (i.e. 10 plus miles). Also, try for softer surfaces if you can, unpaved rather than paved, as this will protect your joints and lessen the harmful impact of foot striking hard surface.

Incidentally, a plateau occurs when you are doing what you did but are no longer seeing the steady improvement you saw before. This is because your body is catching up to the level you have reached, and is not ready for more until it builds heart, lung, bone, circulation, muscle, tendon, and ligament capacity. Just keep training. When your body catches up you'll start to improve again.

But, taking the examples above, once you attain your readily available potential, you will be easily able to do push ups, abdominal exercise, handle the weights, and run the distances at the speed you worked so hard, for so long to attain. And looking back you will wonder at how much time, trouble, and effort it was to do what you can easily do now.

If you are able, and have a place, swimming is one of the best exercises since it involves your entire body and has low impact, but that's a luxury not all of us have available.

Bicycle riding can also add to your exercise regime if you enjoy it but the benefit is more limited to your legs and to some extent your cardiovascular system but adds little upper body strength.

The single best investment in time and effort is martial arts. Once you're adequately conditioned, say 100 push ups, 100 sit ups, adequate flexibility, the ability to run or ride a bicycle for an hour, you should be able to start. This requires a serious commitment, but if you can stick with it, it is the single best physical and mental activity. Just be sure the class is very well supervised and the students are well trained and directed, as serious injuries can result from poorly managed sparring sessions. If the school you attend is poorly managed and you see injuries in sparring it's best to stop attending and look elsewhere. Remember you're using a recreational activity to try to improve yourself physically and mentally, not training for feudal warfare in Asia.

In the above I am assuming you are in reasonably good health.

If you are over 50, have an unhealthy diet (high in sugar, fat, cholesterol, processed foods, sodas), overweight, and you've been sedentary, it's best to get a thorough check up from a physician who can give you a cardiac check up just to be sure you don't have coronary artery disease that's clogged your arteries to the point where vigorous exercise is unsafe. If that's the case you need to improve your condition through proper diet, professionally supervised exercise/physical therapy, and weight loss. The reason for this is that coronary arteries, narrowed by plaque, are adequate for the sedentary body, but exercise like running, swimming, bicycle riding, strenuous hiking, climbing, increases your heart's need for oxygen, requires your heart to work harder, which needs more circulation to perform. The narrowed arteries reduce circulation to the heart, deprive it of oxygen, and causes, angina-the chest pain from a heart being deprived of oxygen, and if you don't stop the stress quickly enough, the classic heart attack, the myocardial infarct, death of heart tissue due to oxygen deprivation, and potentially loss of heart rhythm, which can be fatal. I don't want this for you, and neither do you. Proceed, but, proceed with caution, slowly, under medical supervision. Don't be discouraged, your life depends on changing your ways. Coronary artery disease is not permanent. It can be significantly improved with proper diet and exercise. You'll get there. You'll look better, you'll feel better, and you'll be healthier. And as you improve you'll be amazed at how much better reception you get from women. Women are shallow. They respond well to fit, healthy, strong men. Perhaps it should be that way, and perhaps it shouldn't, but whether it should or it shouldn't, it is that way.

Of all the things you can do to improve your prospects for romance, intimacy, and sex with women who interest you, being physically fit is the most effective.

Intellectual

This is a quality that may not be obvious immediately, but it quickly becomes obvious.

In essence, intelligence is the ability to determine correct from incorrect, to determine what the best course of action is, to understand things, to figure something out, to be able to learn something new, and to figure out how to accomplish something.

You can improve your functional intelligence, and to some degree your brain capacity, by reading, studying, and applying what you learn.

If you read you will improve your speed and comprehension.

If you write anything, movie scripts, plays, short stories, articles, books, poems, reports, a personal diary, you will improve your ability to write, to think, to be creative, and to communicate.

If you memorize you will improve your memory. Say, names, song titles, lyrics, but it could be anything at all. Just make it something you care about, find interesting and worthwhile, that you can master. If it helps you in your work so much the better. I don't recommend spending time memorizing anything that isn't enjoyable, interesting, worthwhile and hopefully, useful to you, but that's up to you. Unless you're in school, in which case you should apply this to your school work.

People tend to have unique aptitudes, such as the ability to memorize and recall, the ability to learn foreign languages, the ability to perform mathematical calculations, the ability to compose music, the ability to write mystery stories, etc. Focus on what you have an aptitude for.

When you study something like a foreign language, computer coding, web site design, etc. not only do you learn something, it helps you to learn better.

If you apply yourself to crossword, scrabble, logic puzzles, chess, or other games, it helps you to think flexibly and practically.

You can actually learn how to learn, how to read faster and understand what you read better, how to strengthen your memory, how to reason, how to think logically, how to solve problems, how to play winning chess, how to write a mystery novel, how to write a three act play, how to write songs, 'how to' do essentially anything and everything.

You may or may not have any more natural intelligence than before you started to study and practice, but you will have more functional intelligence.

Many people we consider intelligent and knowledgable are simply average people who put in time to study each day.

If you pick something that interests you, that you think is worthwhile, that you have aptitude for, and can master, you will look forward to the time you spend at it, and you'll enjoy the time you spend doing it. And if you do this you will be considered intelligent and knowledgeable, and that's a good thing. All women like it if the man they are with is considered intelligent and know-ledgeable, even if she doesn't know, or care, about what he knows.

If you put in even a little effort each day, it will improve you mentally just as exercise improves you physically.

And, as I already told you, for a successful relationship you must be at least as intelligent as the woman you are interested in. So as your functional intelligence improves, you increase the number and intelligence of the women you can have a successful relationship with.

Emotional

Women are emotional. Men can't afford to be. Any man who can't control himself is his own worst enemy. If he succeeds in anything it's despite himself, not because of himself. And whatever he attains will be less than what he could have attained if he had self control.

To be what you should be you must be calm, in control, assertive, courageous, uncomplaining, and manly, strong and gentle, considerate, compassionate, understanding, supportive, and empathetic.

This doesn't mean allowing yourself to be pushed around, or bullied, or being submissive. It's the opposite. Be sure you're right, that your position is correct, take the high ground, then stand your ground.

These are qualities that make you a desirable romantic partner to a woman.

You needn't have these qualities naturally. Some men do, many don't. But all men can develop them. And if you can't, you can project the image of such a man, that is, you can pretend to be such a man, and that generally works just fine for most women.

No one is perfect in all these qualities. You may think someone you know is, maybe even yourself, but if you do you're wrong, because no one is. You can strive to be the best you can be, that's all.

It takes time, effort, thought, practice, and experience to maximize your emotional qualities, but you can, and should, do it.

You can train yourself to master your emotions just like you exercise to build yourself physically, and you study and practice to build your functional intelligence.

Just take whatever comes in stride.

Most irritations and inconveniences are quickly brushed aside with the simple thought: "If this is the worst thing that ever happens to me I'm a very lucky man."

When you set a worthwhile goal for yourself, which you can realistically accomplish, and work towards it, minor matters won't upset you.

If you can accept the worst probable, or even possible consequences, then you will have calmness and courage in action.

Don't be sensitive. You are who you are, and you can't be anyone else. If you suffer rejection or failure, take it in stride, learn from it, and move on. In romance, you don't need to succeed every time, you need to succeed one time.
Remember, there are reasons for everything, excuses for nothing.

Accept fate with good humor.

In success be modest, and in failure, stoic.

When you defeat someone be gracious, and when you are defeated, congratulate the winner.

Never complain.

Everyone has things to complain about, and everyone knows it. But no one wants to hear complaints, and women who interest you are no exception. Women respect stoic men, whom they find very manly and attractive. If you can't take fate in stride, and you feel oppressed by injustice and unfairness, just keep it to yourself. If the topic of some misfortune that befell you comes up, take the attitude that you take it in stride. You got fired from your job unfairly "I'll get a new job, a better one, I know this will come out for the best. Sooner or later something like this would have happened with these people. I'm glad it was sooner. I was wasting my time there." She'll like and respect that. Try to make it sincere, or sincerely try to put on a good act.

You may have taken quite a battering in your life, some of us have. But Thomas Friedman, a New York Times writer said it best: "Don't let the past bury the future, let the future bury the past."

Education

It is necessary to have an education equal to or superior to any woman who interests you.

There are countless women who have the same or less education even if you're a high school dropout. You might think this limits your prospects, but it expands them. Instead of wasting your time with women who aren't going to work out for you, by directing your attention at women, who interest you, who have the same or less education you will have countless women, who will work out for you, from whom you can choose.

If you find that a woman who interests you has a higher, more elite, education than you, move on.

You can, if you wish, involve yourself with a woman of much less academic attainment than yourself although you may find her less than stimulating company after a while.

Just to be sure we understand each other, say the woman is an honor graduate of an elite private school, say Brearley, Chapin,

Spence, and an Ivy League college, Harvard, Yale, Princeton and you are an average graduate of an average high school and college. You have little or no chance, while you could direct your attention to any one of literally millions of women who have the same or less academic qualifications than you.

If you are still in school, or can return, maximize your education. Put in a solid effort to get the best grades you can. Prepare well for the college entrance examination, or graduate entrance examinations, if that's relevant. Participate in activities you find worthwhile in school. Attend the best educational institutions you can. Go as far as you can, and do as well as you can, in a field that you have aptitude for and find worthwhile.

It's the best advise for life in general, but for our purposes, it opens up many excellent prospects you can win over. As you progress through school, not only will you come in contact with many highly intelligent, and beautiful, women of very high character, and winning personality, you will win their respect and admiration by your attainments. And this is just as true if you're the top student at Harvard University or a C- student at a local community college. That's why there are so many romantic relationships among students of the same high school, college, and graduate schools.

If you're still in school, high school, college, and graduate school are three of the best places to meet women who are eager for romance, intimacy and sex. Don't miss the opportunity.

I emphasize, academic accomplishment is relative. Even if you're last in your class at a poorly rated high school there are plenty of women whose academic achievement is equal or less than yours.

Say for example, a man graduates from a local nursing school and becomes a registered nurse in a local community hospital. This may not mean much to a woman who graduated with honors from Harvard medical school and is the chief of cardio-thoracic surgery at a world renowned hospital, but would be impressive to a woman who dropped out of high school and works as a cashier in a store.

But I can't repeat enough, it's your education in relation to the woman who interests you that counts, not anything measurable or objective.

Occupation

You, as the man, must be minimally her equal, which is not preferable, but ideally, higher status, higher power, and definitely higher earning than the woman who interests you.

If you are a nurse and she is a physician, you're getting nowhere, and if your physical attributes attract her, which, if she is available they very well might, the probability of an intimate long term relationship is minimal, and if you do begin a relationship she will likely, sooner or later, find a higher status male more to her liking, and end your relationship. A short term situation is ok if you want it, but don't plan on any long term future. If you are the physician and she is the nurse, no problem.

The higher up you can raise yourself the more women who will find you attractive and desirable.

If you are a nurse there's a huge number of women who don't have status, prestige, power, responsibility, or income that's even close. And plenty of them are beautiful, chic, elegant, and just right for you.

If you want to maximize your desirability as a romantic partner maximize your occupation, normally by going as far as you can in school, doing as well as you can in school, attending the most prestigious schools you can, and concentrating on a field in which you have interest and aptitude.

In terms of an occupation, you can't just be a lawyer, a doctor, an accountant, an engineer, a computer security expert, a teacher, a police officer, a whatever, you must try to be the best you can be, you must try to be excellent, and you must try to gain promotion, because relevant to romance, higher level occupation makes you more desirable to women.

Even if you're a minimum wage worker in an unskilled dead end job it's not an impediment. There are women who have no job and no income, and they're very happy to hook up with a man who has a steady job. Even if you have no job, no occupation, no income, and no money you'll still find women who want to be with you.

It's not a set position, prestige, income, or status. It's position, prestige, income and status in relation to the woman who interests you.

But your occupation is always part of a woman's total calculation. It's unavoidable because all women take this into consideration. But, (especially if you have a high status occupation) be careful of a woman who is interested in you exclusively for your money or status. You'll never be happy with her, and after she gets what she wants she'll stop pretending, and then you'll be miserable until you get away from her, and that's going to cost you. Be suspicious if her looks are superior to what you would ordinarily expect, and her means are considerably less than yours.

Money

It's unfortunate or perhaps not, but romance is extremely hard headed, cold, merciless, follows the rule of Natural Selection and Survival of the Fittest.

In our society, all other things being equal the man with the most money is the most fit as a romantic partner and the one to be naturally selected.

As I explained women want a good provider. That doesn't go

away even if they have high income of their own, and their own money. The desire for a good provider is inherent to their being.

Part of being a good provider is having money, and of course, spending it on them (in an appropriate way within your means).

In so far as romance is concerned you want to maximize your earning power, invest your money wisely, live up to your means, but not beyond it.

You want to be stylish not ostentatious. You want quality not flash.

A man who has at least as much money as she does, and at least equal earning power, is a minimum requirement for most women, although the more he has (in relation to her) the more desirable he is.

But, this is an unspoken rule. The woman who interests you may not even be conscious of this desire, it's so inherent to her being. It's a natural part of the female drive to be provided for.

If you have less there's something about you that makes you undesirable, unattractive, and if you have more, especially considerably more, that makes you exciting and desirable and someone she wants to be with.

Never tell a woman how much money you have. Show it, without showing off. Spend, be sensible and generous, but within your means.

No matter how 'pure' you think her motives are, and how much she likes you 'for yourself' you will discover that she's much more excited by the idea of a romantic relationship with you if she finds out you have a lot more money, or income, (or both,) than she does.

If you do have a lot of money don't flaunt it. That's vulgar, offensive, and unnecessary. Women make it their business to find out how much you have, and how much you make, without your saying or doing anything. It takes women very little time, they are subtle about it, and they won't discuss it with you. You'll find out if you have enough for them because they'll either warm up to you or cool off depending on what they find out.

Of course, this also applies to potential. A female nurse who earns $100,000 will likely be attracted to a resident in say, neurosurgery who makes less, or even a medical school student who has nothing and earns nothing, because in due time he will make vastly more. (His educational attainments are also higher, and his occupational and social status is much higher as well.)

All things being equal (i.e. height, weight, age, fitness, education, intelligence, etc.) a woman will choose a man with a steady income of $200,000 over a man with a steady income of $100,000, whereas her decision would have been reversed if their income was reversed.

If she's considering a relationship with you how you handle money is critical to her long term well being, and she'll watch how you do it very carefully, without letting you know she's doing it. If you waste money, spend foolishly, or beyond your means, that's a serious warning that you're going to impose trouble and hardship on her if she puts herself in a position where she's dependent on you. And, of course, not be a good provider. On the other hand, for a short term blast, a lot of women will gladly go along for the ride, until you run out of money.

Regardless of whatever nonsense some irresponsible people spread around about dropping out of school, by far, across the board, the more prestigious the school you attend, the better you do there, and the farther you go, the more money you will have in life.

Pursue what you find interesting and worthwhile, that you have an aptitude for.

You can do well in anything that interests you, that you think is worthwhile, that you have the aptitude for, for which you get the proper training, that you get the qualifications for, and that you get experience in.

I discourage you from pursuing an occupation solely because you think you can make the most money at it. You'll do well in anything you have an interest, aptitude, and desire for. But if you pursue money alone you'll never be happy and fulfilled. You might think that being happy and fulfilled has nothing to do with success in romance, but it does. When you feel happy and fulfilled by what you work at, and feel driven to accomplish goals you believe are worthwhile, you don't have to say anything to anyone. It will show, and it will make you more attractive and desirable as a man.

And just to be sure we understand each other, 'what is worthwhile', is what is worthwhile to you. For example, most men couldn't care less what women wear, and for many, the less women wear the more they like it, and for most of the rest the less it costs, and the longer it lasts, the better, especially if they're the ones paying for it. But some men are hugely successful women's fashion designers who are passionate about what women wear.

If one of the arts is your passion it's your choice to pursue it as an occupation, and some people, though very few, do make a lot of money at it. But strictly from the point of romance making very little money impairs your prospects. Of course, there are always women who find the 'starving artist' attractive and desirable and want to be with him, but the life you provide would be quite dismal and most women are only too aware of that.

For our purposes, if your interest is knowing how to succeed at romance, the more money you make and have, the more desirable you are to women.

Again I'm going to try your patience: this is relative. Any amount of money is enough for some women while millions aren't enough for others.

So don't live a poor life wasting it getting rich. Lead a rich life. All you need is enough money for your needs, whatever that may be. More for some, less for others. Just be aware of its effect on romance. Whatever you have and earn will be enough for some women, not enough for others.

At the extreme end of the spectrum from those women who are concerned about how much money a man earns and has, as one of many factors (i.e. height, weight, age, attire, grooming, fitness, character, etc.) are women who are primarily, or even exclusively, interested in money. This is an exaggeration of a woman's innate desire for a good provider, distorted by trauma in her upbringing, such as extreme poverty, deprivation, hunger, shame she felt, or was made to feel, over shabby clothes, fear, insecurity, abuse connected to her poor conditions.

There are men who have fooled women like this into thinking they're rich, when they're not, to get a night of sex, or to cheat them out of some money, but the fraud is always discovered quickly. As long as they do it in places like beach resorts, and there's a new group of women every week, they can run this scam indefinitely. One might say it's hard to sympathize with women who get taken advantage of in this way, but taking into consideration where they're coming from, it's hard not to. Whether you do something like this or not is entirely up to you, but, obviously it's not very romantic.

The other group of men who use women's excitement over rich men is rich men who have some interest in gold digging women to get sex, or to otherwise have fun with them in some way. As long as the woman knowingly goes along with this, say, in return for flying to Europe on his private jet, cruising the Greek Isles on his yacht, or staying in his luxurious mansion by the beach, for whatever time he desires before she's dumped, it's fine for both. If you're rich you can do this for your entire life. And some men do. Whether you do this or not is entirely up to you. There's an infinite supply of such women. But again, this is not romance.

Accomplishments And Attainments

Anything you accomplish in life will be meaningful to some women and meaningless to others.

You should formulate an aim, something you would like to accomplish, then try to accomplish it. Select what you can realistically attain and that you feel is worthwhile. Even an attempt at something worthwhile is worthwhile.

Whatever your accomplishment, say running the NYC Marathon, paddling a kayak across the Long Island Sound, serving a term in the Peace Corpse, is of value to some women, not to others (think: "Let's go somewhere quiet where I can get you alone and you can tell me all about it." to "Why would you do that?").

I guarantee you that if you found the cure for cancer but didn't make any money from it, (say, because you did it as a salaried researcher for a big pharmaceutical company) many women wouldn't be very impressed with you, while others would throw themselves at you.

You must present your attainment in a subtle, modest way.

For example: (to the aspiring mountaineer: "I learned more climbing K2 than I learned in four years at Harvard"; (to the aspiring writer: "When I got my first book published I thought I was the smartest most sophisticated person in the country, and no one bought it. Now, after my tenth book, I learn more from my readers than they could ever learn from me."; (to the cheerleader: "People think professional athletes are such extraordinary people. In reality, anyone who's born with certain attributes can be a pro athlete. It's either a person is born with them or a person isn't. No one out there on that field made himself, or for that matter herself, myself included."; the corporate lawyer:

"When I was a beginning associate I made my first presentation to a corporate board. I told them why it was illegal to dump arsenic, mercury, and lead into running ground water, and after two hours of questioning they thanked me for my presentation and essentially kicked me out. I was sure I was going to be killed or at least fired. When I got back to the office the board made me counsel to the board. Now I'm a partner, and to this day, I don't know what I did, or said."; the motorcycle rider: "When I'm riding, I'm not thinking, there's no time, I'm feeling, the road, the terrain, the air, the others on the road, the speed, the force, the balance, right on the edge, exhilaration, where space and time meet in a dimension of their own, and I'm a part of it. There's nothing in this life like it. I know I have to give it up, become responsible, and when I find the right woman, if she wants me to I will give it up, but until then, riding will be my thing, and I just want you to know that."

Never be boastful, i.e. "anyone could do it if they put their mind to it", "it was just luck", "I just happened to be in the right place at the right time", "I can just do it, I don't know why. It just comes easy to me", "I don't deserve any credit, anyone would have done the same thing in the same situation", "I'm just glad I was able to help", "Believe me, I'm no hero. I was scared out of my wits. I just did what I had to do", "If you were six foot ten you could play in the NBA also". Of course, all of these statements are blatant lies, but they'll always work, because they'll either fool the woman into thinking you're a super achiever who is not a conceited jerk like most super achievers, for whom it's all about him, which women don't like, or, if she sees through you, and you are being somewhat of a phony, she'll at least appreciate that you know enough not to be outwardly boastful.

In order to deliver your line in a spontaneous, relaxed way, you have to formulate what you're going to say in advance, not word for word, which would sound stilted and practiced, but the basic points and the order you're going to present them in, then practice, which can even be just thinking your presentation through in your mind until you have it down pat. Once you're well rehearsed you can deliver your lines spontaneously, as if you're telling someone this for the first time.

But, if you can, speak from the heart. Be sincere. You should be modest about your accomplishments. Whatever you've done, it's likely that in the grand scheme of things it's pretty insignificant. Unless you found the cure for a debilitating ailment, or developed a safe effective vaccine, or invented say, safety glass, or brought an end to the cold war, or managed to put through the law that provided food stamp aid for millions of children who were otherwise suffering from malnutrition, or wrote, not a quickly forgotten best seller but an immortal literary masterpiece, it's safe to say your achievements, laudable as they will be to some women, i.e. say, being the umpteenth person to climb up K2 and get down again, you haven't much to be conceited about. If circumstances of life elevate your aptitudes, interests, capabilities and efforts, into an accomplishment a woman you're interested in finds impressive, use it, but don't fool yourself into making more out of yourself than you are. You're as good but no better than anyone else. You can even fool everyone else into thinking you're great, but don't fool yourself. Certainly enjoy whatever benefits your accomplishment brings you, including women, and many men do.

The point is that if you can accomplish something noteworthy it will make you very desirable to many women.

The reason is a little sad. Accomplishing something doesn't make you any better or worse than you were before you accomplished it. You're the same person. But women who wouldn't have been interested in you before are suddenly pursuing you. The reason is that women are excited by proximity to high status, fame, or celebrity. It gives them a reflected glow they bask in. That being with this man infuses her with his 'aura'. In their minds it makes them part of it. All professional sports teams, successful bands, high level politicians, celebrity level actors, even men in the news for say, saving a drowning child, have female fans eager to be with them, without even knowing them. If you have, or gain, status by accomplishing something noteworthy you can take advantage of these women, and many men do, or don't. It's your decision.

Experience

A man who has done, and is doing things, a woman is interested in, is extremely attractive and desirable to her.

Say he has a sail boat and sails it to the Caribbean each Spring, and she loves sailing and dreams of sailing to the Caribbean.

He plays in high school, college, and professional tennis tournaments and she loves tennis and wished she was good enough to play competitive tennis.

He is an actor in movies and she wants to be an actress.

But it can be anything, say playing on a volleyball team, doing trail maintenance, hiking a challenging trail, traveling, going cross country, doing volunteer charity work.

Again, the list is endless.

Having experiences you find worthwhile is justification enough, but experiences make you more attractive and desirable as a romantic partner.

It also brings you into contact with, and attracts, women who share your interests and values. But keep in mind that doesn't suspend all the other criteria. If you meet a woman on a bicycle ride, and you are a faster, stronger, more skillful rider, you have an entrée, but it's of value only if you meet all the other criteria, i.e. height, weight, age, etc. otherwise forget it-but, always, friendly, polite, courteous, respectful, considerate, thoughtful, and positive.

Dancing

Most men don't dance very well, and don't want to put in the effort to improve. There really isn't any reason to bother doing so unless a woman who interests you is interested in having a skilled dance partner. But it is good to be, at least, functional on the dance floor. You can do this with a few simple steps you can master with a little practice, a little experience, and a sense of humor.

That's because most women want to dance at weddings, parties, clubs, etc. So you should be able to dance with her.

There are just a few rules: Don't step on her feet or anyone else's; don't bump into her or anyone else; try to keep to the music-easy for some men, ok for most, impossible for others=but try; don't be self=conscious-no one cares; and, have a good sense of humor.

This is one exception to the rule that says 'Don't do anything with a woman she can do better than you.'

Conduct

Generally we think of living harmoniously, doing no harm, trying to do good, to be a good influence, meaning well. Try to do well doing good. Most, if not all, women respect this approach, so even if you don't feel this way, you would be well off pretending you do.

This does not mean being foolish, naive, weak, vulnerable, in fact quite the opposite.

Stand up for what you believe is right, with courage, strength, intelligence, and fortitude.

Women find men who do so admirable and desirable.

Residence

You should take pride in where you reside, live up to, but not beyond, your means, make it as stylish as you can, reflect your own tastes, be sure it's comfortable and safe, clean and neat.

Make it a place a woman who interests you wants to spend time in.

If this describes your place, ok. If it doesn't, get to work on fixing the situation today.

CHAPTER 14

"The Deal Breaker"

I want to discuss in a little more detail the common problem, I mentioned briefly before, called "The Deal Breaker".

As a man, you should always have respect for the views of others. You should "Agree to disagree" on any issues you can't come to agreement on. But you'll find that most, and probably all, women have these "Deal Breakers".

A "Deal Breaker" to a woman is some point, often of, not only of little, but frequently of no, direct importance to your life or to hers. Example: "What do you think of Black Lives Matter?" (Her father and brother are police officers falsely accused of excessive force allegedly used against African Americans/her completely blameless African American best friend from childhood was shot to death by police in her company); "What do you think of allegations of child abuse by priests of the Catholic Church?" (Her brother and uncle are priests both of whom were falsely accused of molestation/her sister and brother and perhaps she herself were molested by priests when they were children).

Her personal experience has given her a very strong feeling about the issue one way or the other, but, when you're confronted with 'the trick question' you probably don't yet know what her experience has been.

As you see, the problem is, you don't necessarily know what she wants to hear.

As an example of a way you might avoid the trap: if she says:

"What do you think of right to life? freedom of choice?" you know she's asking because the 'wrong' answer is the "Deal Breaker". (Think: her sister was raped at age 14, was screaming in the hospital emergency department that she was going to kill herself if she was pregnant, was given a safe legal 'morning after pill' abortion, and after mental health therapy, recovered from the trauma, that critically, no one outside the family ever knew about, and is now a happily married mother of two/her mother still cries at night over an abortion her mother and father pressured her into, which ended her first pregnancy by the man who became her husband and is her father, who was devastated when he found out about the abortion and still mourns the loss of his first child decades later.)

To you the issue is a complex one with right and wrong on both sides. But not to her.

In reality that issue, as well as every other issue of the same importance, is morally, ethically, legally, socially, and religiously agonizing, with no clear 'right' or 'wrong'. But partisans don't see it that way.

So, taking the example, if the woman who interests you is a "Right to life" or a "Freedom of choice" partisan, which, I think all women are either one or the other, if you're not on her side, she's done with you. Which is a shame in the sense that the issue should never effect you personally.

You know to be responsible, to practice safe sex, and not to risk an unwanted pregnancy. And if you are not responsible, you are unworthy of a relationship, and you remain unworthy until you are responsible.

The same approach to the 'trick question' should always be attempted if you can. That is, sidestep the 'trick question', or even better, get her to tell you her answer. Example: "I've been wanting someone who is intelligent and reasonable to explain both sides to me. Would you explain? I want to learn.". "I don't understand why the two sides are so against each other instead of trying to reason with each other. Can you explain to me?"

Another trick question could be: "Do you support our President?".

Again try to side step: "I don't understand why there's so much vicious attack and counter-attack. Could you tell me?" or "All I hear is argument. I guess I should know more but I've been so busy studying for medical school I haven't kept up the way I should. Can you explain the position of those who support the President and those who oppose the President?" If you can get her talking she'll probably reveal which side she's on, so you can avoid the dreaded "Deal Breaker". After all, what do you care if a woman who interests you supports or opposes the President? (He's not going to win or lose election by one vote anyway.)

In the event a woman who interests you gives you her opinion on something you (silently, secretly, and inwardly) disagree with, I suggest that you simply say "Why do you say that?" without ever being argumentative or confrontational. Then listen to her reasoning.

For most women if you disagree with their opinion concerning something they think is important it's not that you have your opinion and opinions can differ, it's that you're totally wrong, you're reprehensible, you're not her kind of man, and she wants nothing to do with you.

When you deal with the 'trick question' Don't be dishonest, (never be dishonest) but (always) be discrete. With a modicum of good common sense you should be able to avoid the "Deal

Breaker".

If you absolutely have to give an answer to the 'trick question' use the evidence at your disposal. i.e. you met this woman at Sunday morning Mass in a Catholic Church, that she attends every Sunday morning, she dresses somewhat modestly, loves babies and children, shows you pictures of her newborn niece, probably a right to life person; you met this woman in a dance club at 2am, wearing the tightest, shortest, most revealing dress you've ever seen, she had 3 drinks while she was with you (and who knows how many before), went home with you at 5am and had sex the first night she knew you. Probably a freedom of choice woman. But even in these extreme examples, there's no guarantee. Formulate your answer based on the evidence and hope for the best.

But if you are caught in the deadly trap of the "Deal Breaker" and that's the reason a woman who interests you won't see you anymore, just accept that you've lost her. There's nothing you can do to recover. Just move on. But you should analyze how she trapped you so that you can improve your trap avoidance skills for next time.

Perhaps you think it's a little hypocritical to try not to express your own opinion on something just to make headway with a woman who interests you. But, first, it really doesn't matter what your opinion is, nor does it really matter what her opinion is (except to herself), second, there's always right and wrong on both sides of every issue, third, an intelligent pragmatic solution is exactly what those on either side of these issues don't want, and fourth, the real issue is the attitude of the woman who insists that a man be in agreement with her opinions, no matter how rigid, intransigent, unreasonable, and poorly supported, they are.

You could, of course, simply avoid all women who use the "Deal Breaker", but there wouldn't be many, if there are any, left.

You could also express your honest opinion. But if you did there wouldn't be any women left for you because an honest opinion reflects the right and wrong on both sides and this would fail the test of women on both sides. You could try this approach to get a discussion going, and with discussion the chance to escape the "deal breaker".

As an aside, the more rigid the opinion, the less informed, the less knowledgeable, and the less intelligent is the person who adheres to it, and the less willing they are to tolerate any contrary opinion.

When a person is intelligent, reasonable, logical, moral, ethical, honest, and knowledgeable about an issue, that person learns how much right and wrong there is on both sides, and never has a rigid opinion on one side or the other. But if you find a woman who thinks like that let me know, because I never have.

If you insist on finding the perfect woman you wasted your time reading this far. Because there isn't any. On the other hand you're not perfect either. And I say that without knowing you. But then, I'm not perfect either. So let's forgive each other's flaws, try to make ourselves into the best people we can be, and move on.

Women With An Agenda

Remember there are women who might seem to be available to you and are, or aren't, because they have specific objectives at specific times. For example, she's in the hotel bar to meet an NFL player whose team is staying at the hotel; she's at a hospital gala to meet a physician; she's at a South Hampton lawn party to meet a rich guy; so, if you're what she's looking for let her know it-if she doesn't know it already, (if you want to), but be subtle and modest, (i.e. "I guess I look a little funny limping around. Three seasons without a scratch. Then I'm injured in the last play of today's game."; "I guess I look a little pale I've been inside the last two months studying for the boards"; "I'm surprised I was invited. The host and I are bidding against each other on a land deal."). If you are what she's looking for take advantage if you want to. It's usually easy sailing. And they tend to be not only beautiful and sexy but they're ready for action. But just remember, women like this are superficial so there's not much depth there to make a relationship out of. If you're not what they're looking for, i.e. not an NFL player, not a physician, not a rich guy, (and not able, or willing, to successfully pretend you are) don't waste your time. If every woman in the bar is there for an NFL player and you're not an NFL player, no matter who you are you'll get nowhere. Go elsewhere.

Women Who Just Want Sex

Being fit is essential for success with women. The better you make yourself look physically the more attractive women find you to be.

If you get into great shape women will come on to you. Some just want a night of sex. But women who come on to you for sex just because of your great body don't care about you. All men in great shape deal with this. Some men rebuff this type of woman, others take full advantage. When you're in this situation, or work out enough to put yourself into it, how you deal with this is entirely up to you.

"High Maintenance Women"

Like all concepts in romance, it's relative. In this case to what you have.

$5 million isn't nearly enough for a woman who wants to live in a Beverly Hills mansion with private chefs, maids, gardeners, pool boys, and drivers for her $200,000 limo, shop on Rodeo Drive, regularly spend $50,000 on a dress, $2,000 on shoes, wants to fly by helicopter and private jet, stay in luxury villas by the beach, then have you donate enough to get her on the board of some prestigious art organizations. That doesn't mean that while she's got her eyes out for a man who can provide the life to which she wishes to become accustomed she won't spend as much of her $5 million dollar boyfriend's money as she can, because she will. And when he can't, or won't, spend any more on her, he's history. These women are usually stunning beauties, elegant, chic, intelligent, excellent company and charming when they want to be, a sexual experience most men can only imagine, well organized, disciplined, driven, and ambitious.

Climbers

There are quite a number of women who climb from one man to another. They do this because they need a man with money, status, connections, and entrée to gain access to men who have even more money, higher status, better connections, and more exclusive entree. And they use that access to establish their relationship with another man. But given the qualities of women like this there are men who go along when their time with her comes. And she certainly doesn't let on that he's a temporary stepping stone. He only finds that out when he gets dumped for another man.

So unless you think whatever time you get with her is worth it why allow yourself to get stepped on?

Fame, Celebrity, Wealth And Power

Women are excited by fame, celebrity, wealth and power. (There may be exceptions but I don't know of any.)

These women are so charged up they do actively throw themselves at men they perceive as having these attributes.

For some women it's purely physical, they want to surrender sexually, and all men who have any one, or more, of these attributes deal with this.

Some women want to enter the aura and they're prepared to do whatever is required to do so. i.e. "I'm with ....".

Others fantasize about being in a relationship with the man they saw on TV, in the movies, read about in a magazine or newspaper, or in social media, or came in contact with somehow.

These attributes are all relative. So if you have one or more of these attributes and you want to, use it. It makes the going easy. But remember, they're motivated exclusively by what's in it for them.

Women are shallow, but the women who are attracted to a man because they think he has one or more of these attributes have nothing that you can't see.

You are nothing to them. All you are is a professional athlete, actor, celebrity in some capacity. For an overnight she's fine, and in many cases that's all they want anyway.

But if you have managed to gain wealth, fame, status,power, why not find a woman on your level who will care for you as a person and have a relationship with you of romance, intimacy, and sex?

Mental Illness

Mental illness is not feigned. It's very real, and those afflicted with it suffer pain and disability from it all their lives.

Almost everyone has minor issues, such as, say social phobias, shyness, low self=image, unrealistic fears, say, of riding in an elevator, taking a flight, being in a confined space. But this is not mental illness, as long as the person has a realization of the problem.

A truly mentally ill person has lost their grip on reality. They think some evil force is listening in to their phone calls, or has a way to spy on them, or even to communicate directly into their minds, or that an evil force is out to get them, or following them, or that they're morbidly hopeless, chronically depressed, or bi polar.

Most mental illness has periods of exacerbation and remission, and some forms can be controlled with medication, but mental illness is incurable, and it's permanent, a lifetime condition.

Women who suffer from clinically significant depression, anxiety, bipolar disorders, paranoia, neuroses, and Aspergers, will have these conditions all their lives. They can seem quite normal when they are in periods of remission, or when they're on their medication, but they can never be normal.

Mental patients are often extremely intelligent, have excellent memories, excellent recall, can be very observant, even quite charming and delightful during periods of remission. But don't ever be fooled into treating them like normal human beings because they're not and never will be. Many of these people are able to function in society, often on a very high level, think great writers, actors, artists, top executives, leading professionals. but they're still mentally ill. They are found on all levels of society. It's this category of mental patient you will encounter if you meet enough women.

The most serious forms of mental illness preclude functioning in society so you will probably not come in contact with them in the setting of romance. These women have psychosis, schizophrenia, hallucinations, and autism, in which the mental patient is so divorced from reality they need to be in an inpatient care center. Unfortunately there is no known cure for these conditions, only palliative care.

Once you detect mental illness be aware, because these people are self destructive in the extreme, and they will bring you down with them if you allow it. You can't help them and you can't cure them. Due to no fault of their own, they are not normal, and they never will be.

The best advise is find a plausible reason why you can't have anything to do with them, and present it in a respectful, thoughtful, and considerate way. But, have nothing to do with them. Now, what you do, if and when you encounter a mental patient is up to you.

Alcoholism

It's unlikely you'll become involved with a full blown alcoholic because, because not only are they mentally and physically impaired, they're not functional in society. You may encounter a female alcoholic, but if you do, there's nothing you can do for them, they have to have the desire and will to help themselves. So just move on. (Of course, if the alcoholic is a member of your family, or a friend, you will do everything in your power to persuade them to get help. But that's not what we're talking about.)

The only known hope for alcoholics is AA (Alcoholics Anonymous) whose program has been found to be highly effective. Once completing the course cured alcoholics don't have any alcohol at all, even one sip.They are cured so well they can go to bars, cocktail parties, or dinners where everyone else is drinking alcohol and they're fine. Should you encounter a woman who is a former alcoholic, successfully treated with the AA you are safe to proceed. They are completely normal positive human beings.

There are heavy alcohol drinkers, who drink to intoxication, who are completely functional and who are not alcoholics. Many drink to excess only on weekends or holidays, never when they need to be sober. But when you detect this type of behavior, unless you share in it, which you shouldn't, the situation is hopeless. Most of these people deny, even to themselves that they have a drinking problem, and while it's not healthy, perhaps it's a lifestyle choice and they don't have a problem. Most of these people have their alcohol consumption under good control, but on the other hand, it is likely a permanent life time condition. So be aware of what you're letting yourself in for.

Be aware, if you are not, that it is a felony punishable by imprisonment to have sex with a woman who has passed out, or is so intoxicated she is incapable of consent, regardless of the circumstances, or the man's relationship to her. Non consensual sex, meaning sex without affirmative consent, is considered in law to be rape, and it is even legally possible for a husband to be convicted of non consensual sex with his own wife. If convicted a man will be registered as a sex offender, which identifies him and accompanies him wherever he goes, restricts where he is able to go, where he is able to reside, and what he is able to do, even after he is released from prison. On the other hand there is no prohibition from having sex with a woman who has consumed alcohol. She just has to have sufficient awareness of what's going on, and has to consent. Consent is more a legal term than a practical concept. As a practical concept consent runs the gamut from a woman being eager, even taking the initiative, to willing, to passive acquiescence, but the critical point is that she can refuse if she wants to but she knowingly and willingly does it. If you're not completely sure of her mental state, or if she's in and out, don't do it. But see her home safely.

Threats/Bullying/Violence/Exclusion

People use what they have to get what they want.

As you become desirable and effective dealing with women you may run into conflict with men who are less desirable and effective than you are.

Whenever two or more people want the same thing at the same time there is competition. If two or more men are interested in the same woman there is competition.

Since, in many cases you will be more desirable to her than your competition, you may find that your competition may use what they have, the ability to use threats, violence, or exclusion against you.

In Hollywood movies the virtuous hero prevails. In real life the virtuous hero gets a pounding. So use extreme care. In the event of an encounter be calm, non-confrontational, stand your ground, have courage, and show no fear. This type of predator feeds on fear and submissiveness.

The better able you are to successfully defend yourself the less likely it is that a person with the inclination to try to win over you by force will try to do so.

The more fit, the stronger, and the better trained, the less the chance of anyone trying to victimize you.

Martial arts training is the best way, not just to defend yourself, but even more important to discourage an attack in the first place.

The other technique is to exclude you. The most notorious examples are college fraternities who invite women to social events in which they exclude men who are not members, so they don't have to compete with them. The women are often, but not exclusively, members of partner sororities. (The advantage to the sorority members is that they have access to men without com-petition from non member women.) But this is a tried and true technique of clubs and even informal groups. There's really noth-ing you can, or should, do about this. If you are in the included group just take advantage, and if you're in the excluded group just find other women. Of course you could create and carry out the same type of exclusionary group and use it to exclude men who might compete with you, but why bother? If a woman doesn't prefer you to others, move on and find one who does.

CHAPTER 15

YOUR CHOICE

As you can probably tell by now, romance has another inherent, unavoidable problem.

Because women who find you attractive and desirable and want to be with you are not only shorter, lighter, and younger, they're generally less athletic, less intelligent, less educated, less sophisticated, less experienced, less capable, earn and have less money, have lower status occupations, so you are normally having relationships with women who are not only not your equal but are distinctly inferior.

All people are equal in dignity, in their right to respect and good treatment. But that doesn't mean that any two people are equal in anything. They're not. And the criteria I mentioned are the qualities in which a woman who is interested in you will, at best, be equal to you, but more often inferior (remember, not as a human being, but in the specific area).

You may have qualities that complement each other, and despite the differences you may get along quite well. For example many people are complementary in the sense that one has a great memory, but the other is better at problem solving. One might be able to break down a puzzling situation into its parts, the other might see the way to solve the problem. You might be more detail oriented she might see the big picture. You might be a faster stronger runner, but she may be fast enough and strong enough to be a pleasant running companion. You might be able to beat her at chess every time you play, but she might come up with unexpected, challenging, strategies that make the games exciting.

But unfortunately if the woman is so far inferior in intelligence, you get to the point that it's not interesting to talk to her, she has such a limited view of things it's not enjoyable to be in her company. If she's much inferior to you it may not be enjoyable for you to do things with her, say bicycle ride, run, surf, tennis, golf, whatever. She's just so un-athletic doing these things with her is just not rewarding.

So it's the same numbers game. You may find that the first woman who interests you is perfect for you. But it's far more likely that you'll start dating women who find you attractive and desirable and want to be with you, but the more time you spend with them the less time you want to spend with them. In this case it's always better to either settle into a mutually agreeable situation, say, companions for running five miles in the park and having breakfast on weekends, going to the opera, dating once in a while, or just end it altogether.

Two provisos:

If you continue a limited relationship, which can be terminated by either at any time, she understands and agrees. You might be very surprised that, if you want that, she wants it also. Example: you want her as a running companion, she wants you as a running companion; you want her to join you in a subscription to the opera, she wants you to join her in a subscription to the opera, etc.

If you are ending your relationship with a woman who finds you attractive and desirable and wants to be with you, do so with consideration, thoughtfulness, and empathy. She should think even more highly of you after you break up with her than she did before. She should be glad she spent time with you. And she should think well of herself.

Following The Principles of Romance you will be in control and dominate the situation. Use your dominance and control wisely and well.

Summary

You can't tell a woman to trust you or to admire you. You must make her think it for herself. You cannot tell a woman that you have excellent qualities, you must show her, so she perceives them, and thinks for herself that you have them.

Before you can get the part of romantic partner, you must look the part: (height, weight, age, attire, grooming, your perceived ability to protect and provide, your apparent intelligence, your education, occupation, residence, standing, money, interests; and act the part: your desirable personal qualities, strength and gentleness, assertiveness, decisiveness, consideration, thoughtfulness, empathy, supportiveness.

To sustain your romantic relationship you must act the part.

It's never just that you want to be with her, it's that you have to make her want to be with you.

CHAPTER 16

I include this solely because omitting it might cause misunderstanding.

I don't feel that love has anything to do with romance, intimacy, or sex. It certainly isn't necessary for any of that. It could go along with these things, but the presence of love wouldn't enhance, and the absence of love, wouldn't detract from romance, intimacy, or sex.

I would liken it to what I hope is an ok parallel.

A priest hates the church, hates his congregation, and hates everyone in it. But he's a masterful priest, inspiring people to live better lives with moving sermons, counseling with consummate skill and effectiveness, putting people who have strayed back on the right course with the way he handles confession, comforting bereaved, and restoring hope and faith to those who were lost. Another priest loves the church, loves his congregation, and loves every individual in it. But his sermons make no sense, leaving everyone bewildered, his counseling is worse than not being counseled at all, his manner in confession worsens the problems people come in with, his intervention in funerals is devastating, and he causes those who have hope and faith to lose it. How God might judge them I cannot definitely say, but I think God would accept them both. But as to their ministry one is a success and the other a failure. (Of course a priest could succeed in his ministry and also love his church, his congregation and everyone in it.)

If you love, or if you don't, you can have a relationship of romance, intimacy, and sex.

It has been said that a man can make a woman love him, and that a woman can make a man love her. And perhaps that is so.

Perhaps love simply arises between people. And perhaps following The Principles of Romance causes love to arise between a man and a woman.

Perhaps your strength and gentleness, consideration, kindness, caring, thoughtfulness, protection, support, generosity, attention, supportiveness, interest, and loyalty, makes a woman who is perfect for you love you. And perhaps makes you love her.

But I cannot quantify love for you, nor can I teach you how to make a woman love you, nor can I teach you how to make you love her.

So I leave this entirely to you, and to the woman with whom you have formed your relationship of romance, intimacy, and sex.

CONCLUSION

You now have knowledge, and you will soon be prepared, if you devote the time, effort, and thought.

Using your knowledge, being prepared, you begin getting experience by approaching women who interest you, engaging in introductory conversation, moving on to another one, or pursuing her, deepening or ending a relationship, and establishing, or not establishing a bond.

And with experience you gain skill, until you're relaxed and natural. Finally reaching the spontaneity you can only master when you're well rehearsed.

Have fun with it. Don't take yourself too seriously. Because you built up a muscular well built appearance doesn't make you a saint. You're the same person you were before you started your exercise regime. What you've changed is that more women find you attractive and desirable and want to be with you. And when you use what you learned they'll find you irresistible.

You learned what you have to do to succeed and you do it.

You earn your success so enjoy it.

Whether you find the perfect woman for you and form a permanent relationship with her or date an endless succession of women is entirely up to you.

But if you decide you want a relationship of romance, intimacy, and sex, by making yourself into the man a woman dreams of, you will be the man who steps out of her dream into her reality, and, if you choose wisely, she will be the woman who makes your life into a dream.

I would say Good Luck, but luck is not a strategy, and there's no luck involved.

It's entirely up to you.

So, I say, I wish you, and the woman you're in a relationship with, the best.

And this is certainly not the end, it's:

THE BEGINNING